MW00785792

THE JOSHUA PORTRAIT

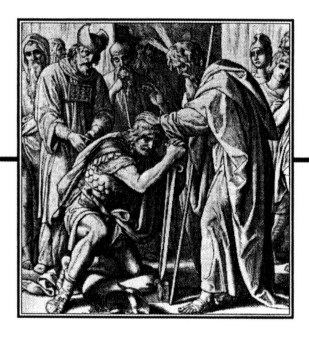

A STUDY IN LEADERSHIP DEVELOPMENT, LEADERSHIP TRANSITION, & DESTINY FULFILLMENT

Kathrine Haubert
Bobby Clinton

Joanna Kratzer

ISBN 1-932814-21-3

Copyright © June 1990 Katherine Haubert, Bobby Clinton All Rights Reserved

Published by Barnabas Publishers

No part of this book may be reproduced or transmitted, in whole or part, including illustra-
tions, in any form or by any means, electronic or mechanical, including photocopying, record-
ing, or by any information storage and retrieval systems, except as is permitted by sections 107
and 108 of the U.S. copyright law and as is permissible for published public reviews, without
permission in writing from the publisher.

Barnabas Publishers
P.O. Box 6006
Altadena, CA 91003-6006

Printed in the United States of America

Cover Design & Page Layout by D.M. Battermann

"He left nothing undone
of all that the Lord
commanded of him"
Joshua 11:15

Table of Contents

Preface

This booklet is one of a series of leadership selection process studies. Leadership selection is a lifetime process in which God interacts in the life of a leader to

- point out potential for leadership (focuses on integrity)
- develop that potential in the leader,
- guide that leader into service; and
- use that leader for His own purposes.

A leader may be born with potential to lead, but it is God who processes that leader so that the potential is realized. Opportunities, experience and training (formal, nonformal and informal) all combine with giftedness to make a leader. And God is active in the whole process.

The major events, people, circumstances, crises, etc. through which God works to develop, guide and use a leader are called process items. The ideas of leadership selection and process items are described fully in Bobby Clinton's self-study text called "Leadership Emergence Theory. Definitions of process items from that book which apply to this study are included in Appendix A at the end of this study. The "Leadership Emergence Theory" book is available through Bamabas Publishers.

The series is broken up into three major categories:
1. Bible Characters   This study is one of these

        a. mini-data studies
        b. midi-data studies
        c. maxi-data studies

2. Historical Christian Leaders

3. Present Day Christian Leaders Studies done thus far in the series include:

Bible Characters	**Historical Leaders**	**Present Day Leaders**
Jephthah	Watchman Nee	Many
Daniel	J.O. Fraser	
Joseph		
Bamabas		
Titus		

Summary Sheet

Person Studied: Joshua

Direct Data: See Appendix B

Indirect Data: Gen. 50:25; Nu. 1:10; 2:1; 10:22; I Chr. 7:26 (Joseph and Elishama); Gen. 48; Nu. 26:28; I Chr. 7:20-22; Hos. 11:3 (tribe of Ephraim); Ex. 7-17:15 (early leadership lessons)

Abbreviated time line:

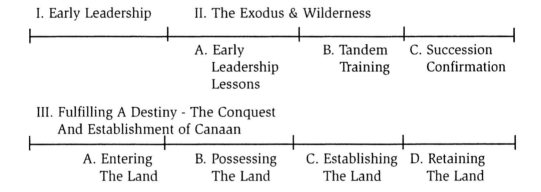

Roles: Slave, Aide, Commander, Administrator, Statesman, Spiritual Advisor

Sphere of Influence: Direct Tribal and National
Indirect National and International
Large Organizational

Major Contributions:

1. Joshua provides a good biblical model for leadership development under mentoring influence. A comparison between Moses and Joshua is helpful along this line particularly when looking at key leadership acts and events. Such a comparison reveals possible effects of mentoring on future leadership.

2. Successful leadership transition can be analyzed by studying the Joshua Model. Many valuable transition principles can be drawn from the biblical text and inferred by historical reconstruction of events.

3. Joshua is a biblical paradigm of destiny fulfillment leadership. A pattern emerges as his life unfolds, giving keys for opening doors to personal and corporate destinies.

WHY WE CHOSE TO STUDY JOSHUA

Joshua's life provides a unique leadership model worthy of investigation. Our desire to analyze his life arises from varied interests and expectations concerning such a study. These interests and expectations are listed below.

1. The spiritual dynamics of Joshua's life are of interest to me. I'm particularly interested in the principles of spiritual warfare and faith that are exemplified in his life (Katherine).

2. Because Joshua's developmental stage was quite extensive, I expect to discover useful items regarding leadership emergence (Katherine).

3. Since the transition from Moses to Joshua was one of the few biblical models of successful leadership transition, I expect to uncover important keys for facilitating this type of change (Katherine, Bobby).

4. Joshua's leadership into destiny fulfillment is another hook in my curiosity. Why did God choose him for this task? What qualities qualified and enabled him for this particular job? How does God move a people (church, parachurch, nation) into destiny fulfillment? How does God do the same for an individual? These are all questions that have perked my desire to study his life (Katherine).

5. What can I learn about Joshua's spirituality? I have previously thought of Joshua as a military leader and Eleazar as a spiritual leader during the conquest of the land. I want to look more closely at Joshua's spirituality (Bobby).

6. Few leaders finish well. Joshua was one who finished well. What can be learned about finishing well? I hope to get some principles from Joshua's life concerning this (Bobby).

How to Use This Study

This study is an analysis of leadership processing that occurred in Joshua's life. For analysis purposes, his life has been divided into phases and sub-phases. These divisions follow the biblical chronology of his life. However, the actual process items found within each division are not chronologically ordered. In each sub-phase the process items are listed in the order they're found on the LSP Overview and Detailed Phase Chart for that section. A discussion of one process item might include a number of different events in Joshua's life. For this reason it is helpful to read the scripture references cited. Also, a glossary of terms is included in the back of this study for easy reference.

Chart 1
LSP Overview Chart A & B: Capsule of Joshua's Life

Development Phase	I. Life in Egypt – A Leadership Heritage	II. The Exodus and Wilderness Experience	III. Fulfilling a Destiny – The Conquest and Establishment of Canaan
Time Span	45 Years	40 Years	25 Years
Geography	Egypt	Egypt/Wilderness	Canaan

	Early Life
	•P(EC) P(CXT) P(FI) P(DP)
		A. Early Leadership Lessons
		1. Encounters with Pharaoh (Ex. 7-12:31)
		  •P(CXT)
		2. The Exodus (Ex. 12:31-14:31)
		  •P(CXT)
		3. At Marah (Ex. 15:22-27)
		  •P(CXT) P(NEG)
		4. Divine Provision (Ex. 16)
		  •P(CXT) P(NEG)
		5. At Massah & Meribah (Ex. 17:1-7)
		  •P(CXT) P(NEG)
		B. Tandem Training
		1. At Rephidim (Ex. 17:8-16)
		  •P(MT) P(AI) P(LI) P(PP) P(NP) P(M)
		2. On Mt. Sinai (Ex. 24:9-18)
		  •P(DP) P(RI) P(SAD) P(I) P(M)
		3. Confronting Idolatry (Ex. 32:15-35)
		  •P(AI) P(CR) P(M)
		4. In the Tabernacle (Ex. 33:7-11)
		  •P(SAD) P(M)
		5. Within the Camp (Nu. 11:24-30)
		  •P(RI) P(M)
		6. Spying Out the Land (Nu. 13, 14)
		  •P(MT) P(RI) P(SAD) P(MSI) P(CR) P(DR) P(FCHG) P(DA) P(M)
		C. Succession Confirmation
		1. Succession Selection (Nu. 27:12-23)
		  •P(LCOM) P(MSI) P(M)
		2. Moses' Speech (Deut. 3:21-29)
		  •P(DR)
		3. A Commission (Deut. 31)
		  •P(LCOM) P(WI) P(FCHG) P(DR) P(DBLC) P(M)
		4. The Death of Moses (Deut. 34:9-12)
		  •P(FCHG)
			A. Entering the Land (Josh. 14)
			1. The Divine Charge (Josh. 1)
			  •P(WI) P(LJ) P(FCHG) P(DR) P(DA)
			2. The Spies (Josh. 2)
			  •P(FCHG) P(DA)
			3. Crossing the Jordan (Josh. 3)
			  •P(WI) P(SAD) P(FCHG) P(DF)
			4. Memorial of Ston
			  •P(OC)
			5. Circumcision at Gilgal (Josh. 5:1-12)
			  •P(OC)
			B. Possessing the Land (Josh 5:13-12:24)
			1. Captain of the Host (Josh 5:13-6:5)
			  •P(SAD) P(DR) P(POWER) P(DA)
			2. Capture of Jericho (Josh. 6:6-27)
			  •P(FCHG) P(MAF)
			3. Battle at Ai & Defeat (Josh. 7)
			  •P(RI) P(SAD) P(PC) P(CR)
			4. Battle at Ai & Victory (Josh. 8:1-29)
			  •P(SAD) P(FCHG)
			5. Reading the Law on Mt. Ebal (Josh. 8:30-35)
			  •P(LI)
			6. The Gibeonites (Josh. 9)
			  •P(WC) P(FLESH)
			7. Victory over Allied Leaders (Josh. 10)
			  •P(WI) P(PP) P(CR) P(MAF) P(DF)
			8. War Wrap-Up (Josh. 11)
			  •P(WI) P(CR) P(MAF) P(DF)
			9. Itemization of God's Goodness (Josh. 12)
			  •P(MAF) P(DF)
			C. Establishing the Land (Josh. 13-22)
			  •P(IRD) P(IMD) P(DF)
			D. Retaining the Land (Josh. 23-24)
			  •P(DF)

Roles	slave	aide/military commander	commander/administrator/statesman/spiritual advisor
Sphere of Influence	family/tribal	local direct national/international	direct local/national/large organizational indirect national/international

CAPSULE OF JOSHUA'S LIFE

The biblical narrative weaves a colorful tapestry that emerges as *The Joshua Portrait*. This portrait is woven with the fiber of life experiences, human responses, and divine initiative. A close-up view reveals many intricate strands unique in themselves and yet somehow interrelated. An overall observation discloses a stable leader of faith, courage, and obedience. This tapestry of one man's life is a statement of divine handiwork. It is the portrait of a leader, the life of Joshua.

Completion of this divine tapestry Joshua's life) took many years, for Joshua lived to be 110 years old. This 110 year span can be divided into three successive periods: 1) Life In Egypt - A Leadership Heritage (45 years); 2) The Exodus and Wilderness Experience (40 years); and 3) The Conquest and Establishment of Canaan (25 years).[1]

Life In Egypt - A Leadership Heritage

Joshua spent his early years in Egypt. He knew the rigors of life as an oppressed minority in a foreign land. He experienced all that the Israelites had experienced: slavery and life under foreign rule. This lifestyle imprinted its early lessons and exerted its formational pressure upon him.

In spite of this humble background, a rich heritage marked Joshua's beginning. His original name was Oshea (meaning salvation). He came from a prominent family in the tribe of Ephraim, a descendant of Joseph (Nu. 13:8). His father's name was Nun and his grandfather's, Elishama. Elishama was captain and head of the tribe of Ephraim (Nu. 1:10; 2:18). According to Numbers 2:18 Elishama was still living at the time of the Exodus and, therefore,

---

1.The number of years for each period is an approximation. Commentators vary on their conclusions regarding dates and time spans

marched at the head of his 40,500 people. Quite naturally his son, Nun, and his grandson, Joshua, would have had a significant place beside him. A Jewish tradition assigns Miriam, the sister of Moses, as his mother (Geikie 1896:126).

The Exodus and Wilderness Experience

It was in the second period of his life that Joshua was prepared as a leader. Thispreparation occurred during the Exodus and Wilderness Experience.

The Exodus

[handwritten margin note: Unaware of direct link to Joseph]

In the Exodus, the tribe of Ephraim was charged with carrying Joseph's coffin from Egypt (Gen. 50:25; Ex. 13:19). It is not hard to imagine how this great departure must have impressed the son of Nun.

Such a situation may well have inclined Joshua to a heroic spirit. We can imagine him, in the prime of life, proudly marching with his father and aged grandfather alongside Joseph's catafalque, at the head of Ephraim's thousands as the great throng left Egypt for the Promised Land. In Joshua's veins coursed the blood of Joseph. Joshua, no doubt, longed to live up to his remarkable heritage. God, then, had long been at work on Joshua's psyche, preparing him for the great responsibilities to come (Hughes 1987:10).

There was a sense of heritage in this man. Joseph's faith challenge in Genesis 50:25, 26 was probably a living burden upon his tribe.

The events of the Exodus did at least two things for Joshua. First, they demonstrated the authenticity, reality, and power of God. The ten power encounters with Egyptian gods, in which Jehovah (through Moses) demonstrated His power, gave renewed hope in the unseen Yahweh. The Red Sea incident culminated this demonstration. Second, these events gave Joshua a leader to whom he could look as God's representative. That leader was Moses, one upon whom the hand of God rested. It was to this life-model that the budding leader was drawn.

Within a month after the Exodus, Joshua was leading the military forces which fought with the Amalekites. Certainly his background accounted for this initial, rapid rise to leadership and his favor with Moses.

The Wilderness

How did God transform Joshua into the leader who would take several million people into Canaan and conquer it? It was the transforming wilderness experiences, or spiritual benchmarks, which fashioned him into a leader. Each of these benchmarks imparted important leadership lessons which affected his leadership character, skills, or values. These experiences include the following:

1. Preparation Through Early Leadership Lessons (Ex. 15:22-37;16;17:1-7)
2. Preparation At Rephidim (Ex. 17:8-16)
3. Preparation On Mount Sinai (Ex. 24:9-18)
4. Preparation Through Confrontation (Ex. 32:15-35)
5. Preparation In the Tabernacle (Ex. 33:7-11)
6. Preparation Within the Camp (Nu. 11:24ff)
7. Preparation In Spying Out the Land (Nu. 13,14)
8. Preparation In His Succession Selection (Nu. 27:12-23)
9. Preparation Through Moses' Speech (Deut. 3:18-29)
10. Preparation Through His Commissioning (Deut. 31)
11. Preparation Through the Death of Moses (Deut. 34:7,8)

Throughout this extensive development phase Joshua was being prepared to step into position as leader of a nation. For forty years he served in a leadership role as one under authority. All along the way he maintained the posture requisite for successful growth and development, a sensitive learning posture. 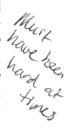 The seeds of an administrator grew like tender shoots as he carried out the details of his visionary mentor's dreams. The embryo of a leader developed into maturity as leadership opportunities provided the exercise necessary to develop inner muscle and outer skills. Faith blossomed in the rich soil of God's word, faith challenges, and ministry successes. The divine testing process was observed (Ex. 17:8-16; Nu. 13,14). The importance of supportive roles was emphasized, and ministry structures clarified (Ex. 17, 18). Foundations for spiritual life were laid (Ex. 24,33). And confirmation of God's purposes were given (Nu. 27; 32:12; Deut. 318-2931). All of these were accomplished under the protective canopy of Moses' oversight. Joshua, the leader, emerged as a product of sovereign intentions, life experiences, and quality mentoring through Moses.

Fulfilling a Destiny - The Conquest and Establishment of Canaan

Joshua began well. At Moses' death Joshua became the head of the nation. Moses ensured that there was a good leadership transition (Deut. 1:38; 3:21,22; 31:3ff). The divine charge gave Joshua the spiritual authority he needed and a sure sense of destiny (Deut.31:15,23 Josh. 1).

The stable stepping stones of continuity also provided for this successful shift from Moses to Joshua.[2] The stepping stones were God's promises, pres-

---

2. Hollander makes some good observations about maintaining stability. He says that providing a stable environment is a necessary leadership function within a group. organization, or nation. This is done by "buffering" followers. That is, the leader does whatever he/she possibly can to protect the people from becoming "vulnerable to an unstable environment." The purpose of buffering is "to maintain enough stability and continuity to sustain optimism and hope, which are powerful motivators" (*Inheriting the Land* 1978: 15).

ence, word, and people (Josh. 1) (Davis 1988:16-21). These proved to be stabilizers in a time of change, not only for Joshua, but also for Israel. Both needed the continuity they provided. Though Moses was gone, these stepping stones were unchanged providing sure footing for Joshua and the Israelites as they followed their new leader into fulfillment of God's promises.

Conquest of Canaan

Joshua's task was two-fold: he conquered the land (seized the promise), and settled the land (implemented the promise). The first part of his task, conquering the land, took approximately seven years (Josh. 1-12). This conquest is summarized in the following biblical events:

1. The Divine Charge (Josh. 1)
2. The Spies - The Incident of the Scarlet Cord (Josh. 2)
3. The Crossing of the Jordan (Josh. 3)
4. The Memorial of Stones (Josh. 4)
5. Circumcision At Gilgal (Josh. 5:1-12)
6. The Incident With the Captain of the Host (Josh. 5:13-6:5)
7. The Capture of Jericho (Josh. 6:5-27)
8. The Battle of Ai and Defeat (Josh. 7)
9. The Battle of Ai and Victory (Josh. 8: 1-29)
10. Reading of the Law on Mount Ebal (Josh. 8:30-35)
11. The Gibeonites (Josh. 9)
12. Victory Over Allied Leaders (Josh. 10)
13. War Wrap-Ups (Josh. 11)
14. Itemization of God's Goodness (Josh. 12)

During this time, the excellence of Joshua's military expertise shone brightly. The sterling qualities of faith, obedience, and courage arose to meet the challenging task of entering into destiny fulfillment, the Promised Land. The quality of previous preparation was being proven in the crucible of experience. An early stage of convergence was taking place. Joshua's role fit many of his abilities and acquired skills. His influence was expanding and an appropriate power-mix was being utilized. He exercised spiritual authority, legitimate authority, and competent authority. He was in the right place at the right time, using a broad spectrum of his potential. Mistakes were made (Josh. 7,9), but the victory was won and the long-awaited promise was being attained.

Establishment of Canaan

The second task was more gradual and could have covered up to eighteen years.[3]

This task, the settlement of the land, can be divided into two stages:

1. Establishing the Land (Josh. 13-22)
2. Retaining the Land (Josh. 23, 24)

At this time, the aggressive conqueror became the stabilizing director of national affairs. The glory of the conqueror became the maintenance of the administrator. This shift in Joshua's role was a necessary key to completing destiny fulfillment. The role changed with the need. The conqueror had fulfilled his task. Now the administrator was needed to establish the people in the land of promise.

Land reform was initiated. The land was distributed in three orderly phases (Josh. 13,15,16,18,19). The strategy for land development was implemented (Josh. 17:17,18; 18:4,5). Kinship associations were established, grouping a number of extended families together "in a way that reintegrated and strengthened them".[4]   Land administration provided for the sub-division of tribal grants according to the number of associations. Protective and military functions were available through these associations.[5] Land surveys took place (Josh. 18:8-10). New areas of people were incorporated into the national system. Tribal territorial claims were arbitrated (Josh. 17:14-18). Social issues were governed (Josh. 23; 24:25-26). And preparations for the future were made (Josh. 24: 14-24).

As his final act, Joshua the spiritual advisor, reminded the Israelites of God's past actions and future promises (Josh. 23). This reminder was sealed with the word of the Lord (24:2-13), a covenant renewal (24:14-24), and a stone of remembrance (24:25-27).

---

3. While there are indications that the conquest struggle lasted longer than the life of Joshua himself, this period of time, from Joshua 13-22, emphasizes the division and settlement of the land.

4. Hamlin claims that the "dan" or "kinship association" (Josh. 13:15,23) is an ancient formula revealing an important part of Israel's social structure.

> "In the Canaanite pattern, the integrity of the extended family, the natural unit of society, was constantly being eroded by debt, slavery, sharecropping, and economic hardship. The poor were being marginalized. The Israelite kinship association (Heb. mishpahah) grouped a number of extended families (RSV "father's house," Heb. belh-ab) together in a way that reintegrated and strengthened them. Since kinship could be acquired by mutual agreement, marginalized families could thus be integrated into the association" (1983:112).

5. According to Hamlin the associations practiced the "principle of mutual assistance. protected members from financial loss and military harm. Members were protected from losing land titles. Loans were interest free to the poor. And each association provided tribal defense (1983:112-113).

Having himself received Covenant Teaching as the key to successful living on the land (1:7-8), he gave it to the people (24:26), along with applications appropriate to this particular time and place (v. 25). He also established Torah Centers as a means of making the Teaching effective in the day-to-day lives of the people (ch. 21)...19 sending the people away, "every man to his inheritance" (24:28), he completed his assigned task to "cause this people to inherit the land" (1:6) (Hamlin 1983:203-204).

Joshua, who began as a servant of Moses (Ex. 24:13), ended as "the servant of the Lord" (Josh. 24:29). He died, along with his associate priest Eleazar, signifying the complete passing of the conquest generation (Davis 1988:22). His grave, with those of Eleazar and Joseph, witnessed to the fulfillment of God's promise, "I will give you" the land (Gen. 15:18; Josh. 1:3). Joshua died and was buried in the place he had rebuilt fifteen miles southwest of Shechem. Thus The Joshua Portrait is complete.

New Covenant Memorials

Two New Covenant memorials hang this portrait alongside the redemptive tapestry, showing it to be part of a series in the greater, divine masterpiece. These two memorials are Acts 7:45 and Hebrews 4:8.

Acts 7:45 displays Joshua as a vital link in the forward movement of Israelite history. "Having received the tabernacle" literally means, "to receive from one another in succession" (Vincent 1914:483). Joshua was in that line of successive leaders through whom the focus of God's presence was carried from generation to generation.

Hebrews 4:8 portrays Joshua as a prototype of things to come. Joshua, who led his followers into Canaan's earthly rest, is paralleled to Jesus who leads His followers into God's full rest of faith. Believers will enter into God's redemptive promise in the same way that Joshua entered into the Promised Land, through faith. But this typology is limited. The rest Joshua provided was incomplete. "Joshua could only lead his people to their earthly inheritance, while Jesus is the leader" into God's full inheritance (Montefiore 1964:85). Joshua led a select group of people into destiny fulfillment, while Jesus opened the way for complete fulfillment for all people. Joshua was but a shadow of the full reality that would be realized in Christ. He was a temporal foreshadow of the eternal deliverance and overcoming faith that would be made available to all.

Joshua as picture of Christ in OT

Chart 2
Overview & Detailed Phase Chart: Phase1
(Life in Egypt - A Leadership Heritage)

Time Span	45 Years
Biblical Data	I Chronicals 7:26,27 Numbers 1:33; 7:48-53: 10:22
Essential Geography	Egypt
Context/Events/People	In Slavery Tribe of Ephraim/Joseph
Major Process factors/ Detailed Items	FOUNDATIONAL • Contextual (national/local) • Family (indirect heritage/worldview/sense of destiny) • Family (direct heritage/model/influence) • Destiny Preparation (a name given)
Sphere of Influence	Family and Tribal

NARRATIVE EXPLANATION OF PHASE II LIFE IN EGYPT - A LEADERSHIP HERITAGE

Overview

This development phase covered approximately forty-five years. During this time a life foundation was laid. God providentially worked through historical events, contextual background, and family influence to shape Joshua's character. Personality traits were formed, early skills learned, and values inculcated. All of these affected the shape of Joshua's life as he later emerged into maturity.

A major developmental task during this early period was the laying of a leadership capacity foundation. This involved extensive destiny preparation, basic skills orientation, and character formation, as well as precision timing.

Joshua was ushered out of this phase as the result of a dramatic shift. Moses' return from the wilderness triggered a series of events that led to a release from a lifetime of bondage. These events transitioned Joshua into the next phase of his life.

The following process items relate to Joshua's early development:

1. Contextual (national/local)
2. Family (indirect heritage/worldview/sense of destiny)
3. Family (direct heritage/model/influence)
4. Destiny Preparation (a name given)

Process Analysis

Process Item I: Contextual (national/local)

Joshua was born into a dual contextual environment. He was born as a member of a homogenous unit, Israel, within the national Egyptian setting. The broader context displays Egypt at the pinnacle of her political power, influence, grandeur, and luxury (Kitchen 1988:422). A continual flux between

Egypt and Canaan marked this time as one of the most cosmopolitan seasons in her history. Tucked within this broader context was the more immediate context of Israeli life. The Israelites were the working class slaves in Egypt. They were a people who had sunk to the lowest position on the social scale. They had touched the low point of oppression under the rule of Pharaoh.

Several things were happening at the broader contextual level. God was setting the stage for events that would occur over the following 110 years. Circumstances were being arranged so that He would receive glory for Israel's upcoming deliverance. Israel was being diminished in stature and Egypt elevated. Thus, in the Exodus, the least (Israel) would thwart the greatest (Egypt), testifying to the obvious, divine activity in deliverance. God was also preparing Israel for transition into a new environment, Canaan. Transition was already taking place through constant Canaanite contact with Egypt. Canaanite language, culture, and geography would not be foreign to the Israelites. Joshua and the people of God were being positioned for miraculous deliverance and subsequent entrance into the Promised Land.

At the narrower contextual level God was preparing a leader. Joshua was actually an Egyptian Hebrew. While his heritage and identity were thoroughly Israelite, he was born in Egypt and knew the framework of Egyptian life and activity. It's possible that basic language, military, political, and administrative skills were acquired as a result of this influence. Also, some cultural practices were probably adopted (e.g. Joseph's mummification).

At this same level, slavery was a powerful tool in fashioning Joshua's character and perspective. The social implications of being an oppressed minority worked as a positive factor (negative preparation). Although slavery in ancient biblical East allowed for the rights of the oppressed, low class status and hard labor pressed heavily upon him (Judge 1988:1462). The result: the etching of humility and endurance into his character.

Early humility marked Joshua's later life. He was content to be subordinate. He obeyed Moses. He didn't complain, and never had an authority problem as far as the Bible records.

Early humility was enhanced by endurance. Endurance develops in the face of hardship (Rom. 5:3), and is a key to successful soldiering (2 Tim. 2:3). The hardship and deprivations of slavery, along with the wait for God's promises (the years in Egypt) worked together to make Joshua a man of perseverance.

Humility and endurance would prove to be a good foundation for a leader of Joshua's caliber. These twin qualities would enable him to meet the challenges of his future commission. And though he was low caste among the greatest people on earth, the Egyptians, he would become a leader of the greatest nation before God, Israel.

Process Item 2: Family (indirect heritage/worldview/sense of destiny).

Joshua was affected by an indirect heritage. The indirect influences that fil-tered down through generations included an Israelite worldview, and a unique sense of destiny as an Israelite, an Ephraimite, and a descendant of Joseph.

The Israelites viewed themselves as a highly valued people intricately linked to their history. Their nation began in seed form under the breath of divine blessing (Gen. 12:1-3) and promise (Gen. 15). The nature of a blessing signifies the attachment of high value and great importance to another (Smal-ley and Trent 1986:67). God's blessing and promise were the marks of a highly prized people. The Israelites were the ones God had chosen to bless and through whom He would bless others. Thus, Israel was a chosen, called out group distinct from all others, and Joshua was a part of that group.

Israel's history began with, and centered in, Yahweh. This historical link provided Joshua with many faith anchors that went deep into the annals of national life. These anchors secured his identity in the reality of God's word and past actions, and not in his present condition as a slave. While his envi-ronment helped shape him, his worldview enabled him to see beyond this present condition into the recorded past and promised future.

As an Israelite, Joshua had a unique sense of destiny. God's promise to Abraham, the father of the nation, outlined this destiny. The promise included greatness (Gen. 12:2), expansion (Gen. 15:5), and possession of a land (Gen. 15:7). This promise was carried down through the centuries. Joshua lived under its expectation and tension. The slavery he was experiencing had been foretold, along with a subsequent deliverance and possession of a land (Gen. 15). This atmosphere of expectation and promise gave Joshua a general sense of destiny as one among the many people of God.

This general sense of destiny was further enhanced by Joshua's tribal heri-tage. He was of the tribe of Ephraim. Many years earlier Jacob had bestowed the birthright blessing upon Ephraim, the second son of Joseph: "His [Ephraim's] descendants will become a group of nations" (Gen. 48:19). As a result, this tribe occupied a prestigious and significant position. Anyone born an Ephraimite would have been aware of this great heritage and the unique place they held among the tribes of Israel. (See Hosea 13:1)

This tribe also had the care of Joseph's remains. His relies were a constant reminder of his last words: "You must carry my bones up from this place" (Gen. 50:25). Every time Joshua would see the sarcophagus of this important relative, he would be reminded of his future destiny. Someday his tribe would march into the Promised Land carrying Joseph's coffin.

Joshua was probably a twelfth generation descendant of Joseph (Geikie 1896:126). This great leader, and man of faith, must have been an inspiration to young Joshua. They were of the same blood. The possibilities of a signifi-

too strong
no proof

cant future were probable in the light of this significant kinship. Joshua's personal sense of destiny must have been stirred at the memory of remarkable, ancestral destinies.

Process Item 3: Family (direct heritage/model/influence)

Direct heritage involves live bloodline contacts. It was this level of contact in Joshua's life that provided him with a leadership model and channelled direct leadership influence into his life. The scriptures portray Elishama as this key contact.

Not much is said about Joshua's parents, but his grandfather, Elishama, seemed to be a significant influence. Elishama means, "God who hears" (Collingridge 1987:22). This name was a faith statement by parents who participated in Israel's groaning under Egyptian domination, It was a reminder, to all who would hear, that God was listening to their cry. It was a statement of certainty in a time of darkness. Whenever Joshua heard this name, he would have been reminded of God's hearing ear. Thus, he was affected by a grandfather who's very name was a faith seed planted into his life.

A leadership model was also provided. During the Exodus, Elishama was captain of the sons of Ephraim, an army composed of 40,500 fighting men (Nu. 1:?3; 10:22). Joshua was able to observe firsthand decision making, strategizing, organizing, and conflict resolution at a high-ranking level. He shared the inner struggles and private confidences of one involved in prominent leadership. This influence invaded his life. Military strategy, maneuvering, methods, and means were probably common to him.

Elishama further modelled good stewardship. As head of a tribe he was undoubtedly well-to-do, and had collected much wealth during the national departure from Egypt. The offering he brought to the Lord in Numbers 7:43-53 was of great value. Estimations have varied from $1,500 to $4,000 (Collingridge, 1987). This act of reverence communicated two possible messages to Joshua. First, God's dwelling has priority. Second, one should give his/her best to the Lord.

Process Item 4: Destiny Preparation (a name given)

A person's name was especially meaningful in the Old Testament era. It often signified an important event, purpose, or quality. Such was the case in Joshua's life.

Joshua was originally called, Oshea (Hoshea, Hosea). Oshea means deliverance or salvation (Good 1962:996). Later in his life, the syllables denoting God, Jah, were added giving his name greater weight. Thus Oshea (salvation) became Joshua (Yahweh is salvation).

The term Oshea expressed the longings of a nation, and of Joshua's parents, for deliverance. The parental desire and belief for a new day found verbal articulation through the naming of their son. In a sense he was the embodiment of the national longing for salvation. And eventually, through his personage, that longing would be realized.

There was also a prophetic edge to his name. It pointed toward a future purpose. It was a shadow of things to come, a foretaste of the great work he was to accomplish for God. This prophetic dubbing glimmered as a diamond of destiny. Joshua probably became more and more aware of this destiny as he was later thrust into leadership.

Chart 3
Table of Principles - Phase I

Name	Observation	Principle
1. Divine Providence	God was long at work on the national and local level to prepare for events that would occur during Joshua's lifetime.	a. God will use the larger contextual scene to position a leader for destiny fulfillment.
2. Minority Background	Joshua was born into minority conditions as a slave in Egypt.	a. Minority status does not disqualify a person from significant leadership.
3. Hardship	Joshua faced the difficulties of slavery.	a. Those preparing for leadership should not resent hardship (2 Tim. 2:3-6) (Collingridge, 1987:24). b. Difficulties, rightly handled, can produce mature character (Romans 5:3-5).
4. Worldview	Joshua's worldview probably helped him see beyond his oppressive conditions.	a. Worldview affects one's perception of his/her environment.
5. Kinship Blessing	The tribe of Ephraim recieved the birthright blessings from Jacob. Joshua partook of this blessing.	a. Blessings of preceeding generations filter down to a leader.
6. Historical Leadership Model	Joshua, a great man of faith, was a leadership model for Joshua.	a. Historical leadership models are inspirations to subsequent generations.
7. Sense of Destiny	Joshua had a powerful sense of destiny as an Israelite, an Ephraimite, and a descendant of Joseph.	a. The possiblities of a significant future are possible in the light of a significant kinship past. b. A personal sense of destiny can be stirred by the memory of remarkable ancestral destinies. c. A family heritage with a sense of destiny can condition one to expect to participate in that destiny (Collingridge, 1987:25.26).
8. Promise Fulfillment	Joseph declared that Israel would leave Egypt carring his remains. This happened approximately 400 years later.	a. Faith and patience are the keys to inheriting the divine promises (Hebrews 6:12). b. Faith-filled words can affect the destiny of a nation. c. Leaders are sometimes appointed by God as a direct desire of previous generations (Collingridge, 1987:26). d. A desire to see leadership developed in one's family may not be realized during a lifetime (Collingridge, 1987:26).
9. Grandparents	Not much is said about Joshua's parents, but his grandfather seemed to be a significant influence.	a. A leader is not necessarily produced from immediate parents (Collingridge, 1987:26). b. Grandparents should actively involve themselves in producing character in the lives of their grandchildren (Collingridge, 1987:26). c. Children will learn spiritual truth from grandparents (2 Tim 1:5) (Collingridge, 1987:26).

Chart 4
TLSP Overview & Detailed Phase Chart: Phase II
(The Exodus & Wilderness Experience)

Development Sub-Phase	A. Early Leadership Lessons	B. Tandem Training	C. Succession Confirmation
Essential Geography	Egypt/Wilderness	Wilderness	Wilderness
Context/Events/People	Deliverance and Flight from Egypt/Early Experiences in the Wilderness	Israelites Wander in the Wilderness/Joshua is mentored by Moses	The Selection and Commissioning of Joshua
Major Process Factors/Detailed Items	INNER LIFE • Contextual (Conflict/Crisis/Power) GUIDANCE • Contextual (Destiny Fulfillment) • Negative Preparation (Guidance)	FOUNDATIONAL • Destiny Preparation MINISTRY (TRANSITIONAL) • Ministry Task MINISTRY (FOUNDATIONAL) • Authority Insight • Relational Insight MINISTRY (EXPANSION) • Literary Item • Spiritual Authority Discovery • Ministry Structural Insight • Crisis • Leadership Backlash • Destiny Revelation • Faith Challenge • Prayer Power • Networking Power LIFE MATURING • Isolation GUIDANCE • Divine Affirmation • Mentoring	MINISTRY (TRANSITIONAL) • Leadership committal MINISTRY (EXPANSION) • Ministry Structure Insight • Spiritual Authority Discovery • Word Item • Faith Challenge • Destiny Revelation GUIDANCE • Double Confirmation • Mentoring
Roles	Aide/Possible Teacher	Aide/Military commander	Upcoming National Leader
Sphere of Influence	Local	Direct National/International	National

NARRATIVE EXPLANATION OF PHASE II
THE EXODUS & WILDERNESS EXPERIENCE

Overview

The second phase of Joshua's life marked the formational stage. During this time, Joshua was shaped into that individual who would ultimately assume the position as national leader of Israel. While he functioned in various leadership roles, and was viewed as a significant figure alongside Moses, this time was basically formational.

Phase two can be divided into three sub-phases: early leadership lessons, tandem training, and succession confirmation. These successive time-frames were distinguished by different emphases in Joshua's life. The first sub-phase, early leadership lessons emphasized development facilitated by indirect learning experiences and observations. The second one was initiated by the first mention of Joshua in scripture, along with his first identifiable ministry task. Throughout this sub-phase, there was close association between Joshua and Moses. The learner, Joshua, grew and was mentored as a result of this association. The final sub-phase was triggered by God's selection of Joshua as Moses' successor. It was marked, not by leadership acts, but by leadership confirmation. Thus, the Exodus and Wilderness Experience represents a developmental cycle that moved from a transitional time (Sub-Phase A), to a longer, stable season (Sub-Phase B), into a boundary mode (Sub-Phase C).

Sub-Phase A: Early Leadership Lessons

This sub-phase precedes any known historical record of Joshua's life. However, as an Israelite, he was involved in the events during this period. The major process items in this sub-phase include the following:

1. Contextual (conflict/crisis/power)
2. Contextual (destiny fulfillment)
3. Negative preparation

Process Item I: Contextual (conflict/crisis/power)

The contextual factors served at least two purposes: to bring expansion and to impart instruction. Joshua was expanding into the broader purposes of God. The context caused a physical and spiritual movement which would lead and place Joshua into identifiable leadership. In conjunction with this movement many leadership lessons were being learned. Joshua had an opportunity to develop an experiential theology, to learn about authority and guidance, and to recognize the importance of establishing memorials.

The first five incidences that occurred during this time created a context of conflict, crisis and power, the context in which these early leadership lessons were staged. The encounters with Pharaoh represent a series of conflicts which resulted in crises, which in turn were met by divine power (Ex. 7-12:31). The Exodus continued this cycle (Ex. 12:31-14:31). There was ongoing conflict of interest between Pharaoh and God, the resulting crisis between Pharaoh's army and the Israelites at the Red Sea, and the consequent intervention of divine power (the parting of the sea and the destruction of Pharaoh's army). The scenes at Marah (Ex. 15:22-27), the Desert of Sin (Ex. 16), and Meribah (Ex. 17:1-7) portray the same contextual elements. In each of these situations, a crisis produced conflict (leadership backlash), which resulted in divine intervention (prayer power). Thus a high pressure atmosphere existed. The purpose was to move Joshua and the Israelites into the physical and spiritual position necessary for advancement in God's plan.

Throughout this season of change, a theological foundation was being laid in Joshua's life. It was a foundation he would need for future leadership and destiny fulfillment. The occasions evidencing God's power revealed divine protection (Ex. 8:22; 9:26; 10:23), provision (Ex. 11:2;12:35,36; 15:25; 16:4;17:6), deliverance (Ex. 14:5-31), and guidance. Joshua would need an understanding of these divine activities throughout his life, especially during the upcoming years of conquest in Canaan. God's overthrow of Pharaoh's resistance modelled the divine ability to overcome insurmountable odds, odds which Joshua would meet again in future battles (cf. Ex. 17:8-16; Josh. 6). Another lesson came through the revelation of Yahweh as a man of war (Ex. 15:3).[6] Israel experienced Yahweh as "one who acts by fighting for his people himself...who leads the 'war of Yahweh" (Noth 1962:124). This was an early lesson which would be repeated until it was securely fastened in Joshua's understanding (cf. Ex. 17:8-1 & Josh. 5:13-15). It would be basic to his leadership role as military commander, and to his perception of military structure.

---

6. Compare this to similar revelations of God which occurred later in Joshua's life: "The Lord is my Banner" (Ex. 7:15); the name change to "Joshua" meaning, "God will deliver" (Nu. 13:16); "the commander of the Lord's army" (Josh. 5:15); and the Lord who fought for Israel (Josh. 10:14).

The context provided an environment filled with authority insights. Joshua's mature leadership rarely evidenced the type of conflict found in Moses' life.[7] This could imply that Joshua had learned negative authority lessons through Moses. On the other hand, positive authority lessons were demonstrated, such as, the source of authority (God), the purpose of authority (to accomplish God's will and meet the needs of the people), the exercise of authority (in meekness, through prayer), and the power base for spiritual authority (a praying relationship with God).

Divine guidance was another important element. Joshua witnessed God's faithfulness in guiding His leaders through times of crisis. The context, which created a need for divine guidance, served to emphasize the value of incorporating spiritual sensitivity (hearing God's voice) into effective leadership. Also, general assurance of God's guiding presence was given as a result of the ever-present cloud or pillar of fire.

National memorials were established during this time. These memorials of God's power acts were to serve as reminders for present and future generations.[8] The Passover was the first rite instituted (Ex. 12:21-28). It marked the first time Israel was instructed to observe a nocturnal rite (Noth 1962:89). Thus its importance must have deeply impressed Joshua. It would serve as a faith anchor for future redemptive needs. A second ordinance, the Sabbath rest, was also introduced (Ex. 16:22-30). It was a significant destiny item. The Sabbath rest, while ultimately symbolic of Christ, was a foretaste of the rest into which Joshua would led his people (Josh. 11:23; 14:15). Finally, the preserved manna samples were displayed as testimonials of God's provision (Ex. 16:31-36). These memorials would be Joshua's constant faith reminders. As a leader, he'd be required to provide similar faith anchors for his followers and subsequent generations (Josh 4; 8:28,29; 9:30-32; 24:25,26).

Process Item 2: Contextual (destiny fulfillment)

Sub-Phase A marks the beginning of destiny fulfillment for the nation of Israel. God had promised national deliverance from Egypt (Ex. 6:6). Joshua was seeing this deliverance take place. He marched out of Egypt with the Ephraimites who carried Joseph's coffin, an event prophetically foretold years earlier. The realization of direct, sovereign involvement and answered hopes, must have given encouragement in the midst of fearful change and the crises to follow. Experiencing dramatic fulfillment of the divine promises must have stirred and emboldened Joshua's faith. Fulfillment was expanding and prepar-

---

7.The Israelites did grumble against Joshua when he honored his treaty with the Gibeonites (Josh. 9:18b). Joshua was involved in activity, going forward toward a goal versus Moses' wandering, no meaning beyond enduring. Notice a marked difference in the tow leaderships.

8.For additional thoughts on memorials, see the conclusion on "Destiny Fulfillment - Reaching Personal and Corporate Goals."

ing him for future faith challenges (cf. Nu. 13,14). If God did it before, He could do it again.

Process Item 3: Negative Preparation (guidance)

The events at Mara, the Desert of Sin, and Meribah were negative experiences which helped thrust Joshua into the next stage of his development. Joshua was about to move into identifiable leadership, and these events seemed to signal this change (a boundary item). Prior to and throughout this time, Joshua had not been singled out in scripture. However, after these events, he was specifically identified with Moses and seen in noted leadership.

At Marah, the wilderness struggles began and Joshua witnessed them first-hand (Ex. 15:22-27). He observed the test (bitter waters, v.23), the negative response people grumbled, v.24), and the remedial action (Moses interceded and God responded v.25).

In the Desert of Sin (Ex. 16), he faced the divine testing process again. He went through the test along with the Israelites (no food, v.3), observed the corporate response (grumbled, v.2)., and partook of the remedial action (leadership rebuke, vv.6-8, and divine provision of manna, vv.4-5). This incident was a dual testing item. The remedial action itself proved to be a further test (v.4): the provision of manna tested obedience. Joshua was learning about, and being tested in, his attitudes (v.2), faith (v.12), and obedience (v.28).

At Meribah Joshua had his third negative learning experience. These back-to-back lessons must have imprinted themselves upon him by their repetition. Ongoing adverse conditions and relational problems often force dependence upon God at junctures where change in ministry is eminent. This is what happened to Joshua. Here again, Joshua observed the antagonism toward Moses ("why did you bring us out of Egypt?" vv.2,3), saw Moses' reaction (he cried out to the Lord, v.4), and witnessed divine provision (water from the rock, v.6). While Joshua had been learning about God's testings in each of these situations, he saw that a wrong response left unchecked (in the first two incidences) can become a point of major conflict (they wanted to stone Moses, v.4), and a serious spiritual problem (they tested the Lord, v.7).

Joshua was learning many lessons. Flexibility was being kneaded into his character. It's likely that these events produced dependence upon God and willing obedience. Dependence and obedience were necessary requisites to move him into his first recorded leadership act under Moses (Ex. 17:8-16).

Sub-Phase B: Tandem Training

Throughout tandem training Joshua functioned in a subordinate and yet coordinate role with Moses. Moses was his mentor. Many developmental functions and leadership lessons occurred as a result of this relationship. The emphasis was upon tandem training. Joshua shared Moses' learning experiences through modelling, mentoring, and informal apprenticeship. In this way Joshua's advancement took place.

The major process items in this sub-phase include the following:

1. Destiny Preparation	9. Leadership Backlash
2. Ministry Task	10. Destiny Revelation/Confirmation
3. Authority Insight	11. Faith Challenge
4. Relational Insight	12. Prayer Power
5. Literary Item	13. Networking Power
6. Spiritual Authority Discovery	14. Isolation
7. Ministry Structural Insight	15. Divine Affirmation
8. Crisis	16. Mentoring

Process Item 1: Destiny Preparation

Joshua's journey up the mountain in Exodus 24:9-18 was a significant preparatory event. Not only was Joshua included with the many elders who saw Yahweh (v.10), but he also accompanied Moses to the top of the mountain (v.13). Joshua alone received this special mentoring privilege. The bestowal of this privilege was an indicator of the elder leader's confidence in his protege, and hinted at Moses' future expectations for Joshua.[9] Ongoing mentoring was an indication that God's hand was upon him.

The event in Exodus 24:9-18 served to instill a growing awareness of a future purpose. It was an ingredient added to the mix of life to produce firmness to Joshua's sense of destiny. It solidified his awareness of a significant future, and was important in developing leadership characteristics and values.

Process Item 2: Ministry Task

The Tandem Training sub-phase begins and ends with a ministry task (Ex. 17:8-16; Nu. 13,14). In both instances the developmental task involved "identification of leadership potential, and the formation of basal leadership character through testing" (Clinton 1989:313). The testings were aimed at developing Joshua's inner life, and his faithfulness and obedience in tasks that had closure, accountability, and evaluation.

The first incident at Rephidim (Ex. 17:8-16) tested Joshua's leadership ability and potential. He was given the task of selecting men from the tribes to pro-

---

9. An important mentoring principle is Goodwin's expectation principle: "A potential leader tends to rise to the level of genuine expectancy of a leader he or she respects." Goodwin, in his small paperback book, *The Effective Leader*. identified this principal. It has been modified by Bobby to apply to leaders (Clinton 1989:343).

tect Israel against the unprovoked attack by the Amalekites. From a scripturally passive leadership, Joshua was given a very active role. He was transitioning from obscurity (from a biblical point of view) into marked leadership. At this juncture he stood out in public leadership strength. He proved himself worthy of the task at hand. From this point, on he was identified in close association with Moses.

The second ministry task occurred in Numbers 13,14. God was testing Joshua's faithfulness and obedience. Again, the emphasis was upon Joshua's inner qualities. His past experience with the divine testing process (Ex. 15,16,17) gave him a basis for discerning appropriate behavior during this time. His response to this task would be a good indicator of his ability to lead the Israelites into the Promised Land. Had his response not been appropriate, it's doubtful that he would have been chosen, a short time later, as Moses' successor (Nu. 27:12-23). It was a task, adequately met, which led to greater responsibility.

Process Item 3: Authority Insight

Joshua continued to gain authority insights. At Rephidim (Ex. 17:8-16) he knew what it meant to be a leader under authority. While he led the Israelite army, it was clear that responsibility for the outcome of the battle rested upon Moses (v.11). Joshua was acting in obedience to Moses. He was learning about submission to authority, and acquiring insight into authority structures. Men were under him; he was under Moses; and Moses was under God. Within this structure of authority were leadership supports. Aaron and Hur buttressed the highest level of authority, Moses. Joshua would later welcome this type of support in his future relationship with Eleazar (Nu. 27:21). Finally, Joshua was able to identify the source of Moses' authority. This authority came through prayer as evidenced by the upraised hands (v.11). This lesson illustrates the value of spiritual authority as the primary power base.

In Exodus 32:15-35 authority insights continued to unfold. Principles on the exercise of authority were abundant for Joshua to observe. These principles include the following:

1. The exercise of forceful, direct, and immediate authority is appropriate in times of crisis (vv. 20,26,27).

2. Authority refuses to "pass the buck" (Aaron tried to shift the blame on the people (vv. 22-24).

3. Authority is not afraid to act (Moses moved swiftly). 4. Crisis events might require a leader to identify committed followers, and seek an outward show of that commitment (v.26).

This incident also provides examples of two authority power forms: spiritual authority and competent authority. First, spiritual authority was exercised when Moses suggested that alliance to him meant alliance with God (v.26). He said, "Whoever is for the Lord, come to me" (v.26). Second, competent authority was modelled in verses 30-32. Here, authority was the result of Moses' ability to do for his people what they couldn't do for themselves, exercise the spiritual function of atonement.

Process Item 4: Relational Insights

There were at least three incidences in which God expanded Joshua's capacity to understand, value, and establish relationships with others. These incidences are found in Exodus 24:9-18, Numbers 11:24-30, and Numbers 13,14.

Joshua was not alone as a leader (Ex. 24:9-18). He belonged to a larger group of leaders: "Aaron, Nadab and Abihu, and seventy of the elders" (v.9). Among these, Aaron and Hur were selected to decide legal matters in Israel (v.14). In this context, Joshua must have learned what it meant to relate to other leaders, to make room for their contributions, and to function as a team (Collingridge 1987:39).

While Joshua was a leader among many leaders, he was also an aide to Moses (Ex. 24:13). This unique position enabled him to establish a relationship which would develop servanthood characteristics. Joshua was learning how to function and relate as a servant to another. The value of this relationship cannot be underestimated for leadership greatness must be preceded by a servant spirit. Jesus clearly acknowledged this principle when He said, "Whoever wants to become great among you must be your servant, and whoever wants to be first must be slave of all" (Mk. 10:44). Joshua's future held leadership greatness, but before greatness could become a reality, servanthood must be the practice.

The scope of Joshua's relationship insights needed to be enlarged. He was reticent to share the spiritual dimensions of Moses' leadership with others (Nu. 11:24-30). Two elders, Eldad and Medad, prophesied in the camp.

> When the news of this reached Joshua, the servant of Moses, he felt envy for his master's reputation. What would the people think if they found these two men assuming such a leadership as had previously been restricted to Moses? In Moses' answer we see the greatness of the man. He did not envy others who might rise to positions of supremacy. His whole desire was that the work of God should go forward. "Would God that all the Lord's people were prophets and that the Lord put His spirit upon them!" (Blain 1953:176).

Moses modelled the spirit of godly leadership. He wasn't a demagogue, suspiciously protecting his interests. He was concerned for Israel's corporate welfare, and not his own position. He wanted others to share in God's wonderful gifts.

#2 value of people

What was Joshua learning? He was learning that true spiritual leadership knowsnothing of a self-promoting spirit. It displays a zeal for God's glory no matter who is involved. It neither envies nor deprecates the giftedness of others, but rejoices in their accomplishments for God. True spiritual leadership needs others and welcomes their giftedness.

On the other hand, Joshua learned that there are times when relationships must not affect a leader. This thought was communicated through a negative experience in Numbers 13 and 14. The entire Israeli populace, except for Moses, Aaron, Caleb and Joshua, exercised forceful opinions against God's purposes. They did not want to enter the Promised Land, in fact, denied God's claims that they could. It was time for Joshua to resist the impact of relationships on his leadership choices. He painfully learned that the majority are not always right.

Process Item 5: Literary

Joshua was greatly influenced by the writings of Moses. After the battle with Amalek (Ex. 17:8-16), the Lord said to Moses, "Write this on a scroll as something to be remembered and make sure Joshua hears it" (v.14). The margin of the New American Standard Bible says, "Write this in the book as a memorial." "It seems clear that a definite article is used here. There was a book of God which continued to grow, and this became the Pentateuch itself....Early in Joshua's life, therefore, he was in a definite way wrapped up in THE book" (Schaeffer 1975:10). Later, as Joshua was entering the Land, the Lord told him, "Do not let this Book of the Law depart from your mouth...then you will be prosperous and successful (Josh. 1:8). Obviously, this book was significant to Joshua. His interaction with it would influence, and even determine, the course of his life.

God was able to continue teaching Joshua through Moses' writings. Through these writings Joshua was provided with a lifetime of lessons applicable to life and ministry. In this way his mentor's impact was extended beyond their time together. The Book would influence Joshua for the rest of his days (Collingridge 1987:38).

#3 history

The Lord wanted to make sure Joshua knew that the battle event at Rephidim had been recorded (Ex. 17:14). This written record was to be a reminder of God's victory. God was giving Joshua a faith anchor for future tests and faith challenges. It would serve as an assurance of similar victories to come. The written account would be a powerful tool in affecting destiny fulfillment. The Lord wanted this tool securely placed in Joshua's hands. It was a literary memorial that marked the way for God's people. It was a light along the pathway of destiny, and a testimonial to the God whom Joshua served.

Process Item 6: Spiritual Authority Discovery

Throughout this sub-phase, Joshua experienced God in unique and direct ways. In Exodus 24:9-18 he, along with the elders, saw God (vv. 9,10). Up until this time his primary focus had been on Moses and the power of God invested in Moses' life. Here, however, Joshua had his own encounter with the Lord. God was capturing his attention with a heavenly vision. The impact must have been profound as he began to discover the power of God's presence.

Joshua and Moses proceeded up the mountain of God (Ex. 24:13). This unique privilege afforded Joshua the opportunity to sit at God's footstool while Moses spoke to Yahweh.[10]   Joshua was the only one chosen to accompany Moses on this occasion. None of the other leaders had been granted this experience. Because of the unique quality of this privilege, his right to influence was being expanded. He would have more influence, more clout, based upon his selection for involvement in a rare opportunity.

Since Joshua didn't accompany Moses all the way up the mountain, for forty days he was alone in the presence of the Great I Am (Ex. 24:15). He was experiencing a unique relationship with Yahweh. In this relationship he was discovering the springs of true spiritual authority, the umbilical cord of life and ministry. He was tasting the goodness of the Lord. God's hook was being planted in his heart. A God-hunger was being stirred.

In Exodus 33: 11 this hunger continued. Joshua remained in the "tent of meeting." He chose to remain in the place where God's presence was being manifested. A love for the intimate presence of God blossomed, a love requisite for spiritual leadership and authority.[11]

In Numbers 13 and 14 pressure items triggered a desperate turning to God and an experience of glory (Nu. 14: 10). The manifestation of God's glory among the Israelites, validated Joshua's position. God's affirming presence gave him credibility in the eyes of the people. God was backing His leader. Joshua was learning that the fountain of spiritual authority springs from God.

Process Item 7: Ministry Structural Insight

In a military task at Rephidim (Ex. 17:8-16) and in a spy mission (Nu. 13,14), Joshua learned lessons that would be valuable for structuring future military ventures. Organizing people for military purposes had been one of his tasks at Rephidim (Ex. 17:8-16). This would be helpful when making preparations for future battles in Canaan. His involvement in the crucial spy mission

---

10.Joshua was alone with Moses for six days when the cloud covered Mount Sinai (Ex. 24:15). On the seventh day Moses left Joshua alone for forty days (Ex. 24:18).

11.In his book, *Leadership Emergence Theory.* Bobby states, "Spiritual authority comes from a life and a ministry which demonstrates the presence of God.... A leader with spiritual authority knows God and His ways and demonstrates this in life" (Clinton 1989:192).

showed him the devastating results of making it a public venture. He decided to direct his own spy excursion secretly and reaped successful results (Josh. 2:1,24). His spy party consisted of two men rather than twelve as Moses had done (cf. Josh. 2:1; Nu. 13:2). While Moses chose twelve spies in obedience to God's command, perhaps Joshua's recollection of the event (only two spies brought a good report) affected his choice in numbers. After all, two people of faith are better than a company of unbelievers. As a result of these early experiences Joshua learned about structuring and carrying out military expeditions.

Process Item 8: Crisis

Joshua experienced at least two crises during his tandem training with Moses. The first one occurred after Moses and Joshua descended from Mount Sinai (Ex. 33:15-35). During their forty day absence, the Israelites had turned to blatant idolatry. The crisis involved national departure from Yahweh. Joshua was able to observe the situation and make note of Moses' response. The incident was a major test for Joshua and Moses after being in the presence of the Lord. Their holy experience stood in sharp contrast to the idolatry of the Israelites. Perhaps God was testing humility after their lofty spiritual encounter. This event was a pre-test for the exam Joshua would have when he brought a good report from Canaan (Nu. 13,14)

Joshua's and Caleb's good report of the Promised Land set off another crisis (Nu.13,14). Their report met opposition. The upheaval among the people created overwhelming odds against Moses, Aaron, Joshua and Caleb. The pressure was intense. Leadership backlash produced a crisis. The crisis: the people wanted to stone them (14:10). Joshua had seen Moses face these odds many times. Now he would have an opportunity to discover how much of his past observations could be applied to a current situation. Sovereign intervention provided a solution, just as it frequently had for Moses. Joshua's God was big enough to intervene on his behalf. God met him in the midst of his crisis.

A willful intent to stand firm for God carried Joshua through. Firmness in crisis would be necessary in future conquest struggles. God was developing steadfastness in the face of opposition. Iron was being forged in the crucible of crisis and conflict, an iron of character for leadership strength.[12]

---

12. Hollander explains that it is difficult to define specific leadership traits. These traits can vary according to position. circumstances and follower expectations. In his book, Leadership Dynamics. he gives an explanation.

> There are "...varying findings concerning qualities required to be a leader and those needed to be a successful one. Mainly the source for this variability appears to be the different expectations about the functions the leader is to perform. That is why it is necessary to consider the characteristics of the leader as they are perceived to be relevant by other group members, within the demands of a given situation" (1978:23).

Process Item 9: Leadership Backlash

At last the children of Israel were on the edge of promise fulfillment (Nu. 13,14). The Promised Land lay ahead. Twelve men were sent out to access the property. Conquest was the plan. But when ten spies returned with a bad report (13:27-29), the Israelites turned on the leaders who proposed to go ahead as planned (Nu. 14:2). Joshua was among those leaders.

The rise of conflicting opinion produced alienation and isolation. Joshua was tasting bitterness of blame for an action God had ordained. He now knew what it meant to be disdained, to be the object of wrath from those he led. But he maintained clarity of vision and faith, embracing God's word.

The temptation was to obscure the vision that had been clear. Faith was being shaken, but found true. Single-eyed vision would be necessary to follow through during the conquest and settlement of Canaan. The vision of God's promise must not be clouded by opposition when he would later emerge into primary leadership. Faith must be tested and matured before the challenges of Jericho (Josh. 6) and Ai (Josh. 8:1-29) could be met.

Spiritual muscle was being exercised, producing perseverance. Joshua had been with Moses for awhile. He even stood beside him in the midst of difficulties, but now the whip of accusation flailed his own back. Would Joshua hold firm, or would he abandon position? Perseverance was being tested and developed. Unflinching resolve took hold. Joshua would not be moved. As a result, God was spurred to action. Yahweh intervened to affirm His leader.

Process Item 10: Destiny Revelation/Confirmation

Joshua had a strong sense of destiny. There had been a growing awareness that God had marked him out for His purposes. An early indicator of this was his birth name, Oshea. This sense of destiny grew through subsequent experiences.

One of these experiences involved a name change. Moses changed Oshea's name to Jehoshua, or Joshua (Nu. 13:16). This was done by adding the covenant name of God to his name. Thus, the one who had been dubbed Oshea (salvation) was now graced with Jehoshua (Yahweh is salvation).

While it's not certain when this change occurred, it seems likely that the alteration took place in conjunction with a paradigm shift, or an incident demonstrating God's delivering power, such as the battle at Rephidim. Or perhaps Joshua's mentor, Moses, felt the need to impress his protege with the reality of God's delivering power. Whatever the reason might have been the change was significant.

This significance is three-fold. First, the new name was prophetic. Joshua would experience God's deliverance many times in the future. Also, this name is the Old Testament version of the New Testament name, Jesus. This suggests that his life, in some way, would portray Christ and His redemptive work. And indeed, Joshua did become a part of the scarlet thread of redemption woven throughout scripture.

Second, his new name was a faith challenge. It represented a challenge to Joshua, a challenge to take steps of confidence based on God's ability. It's no accident that this name change was introduced in context with what was conceivably the severest test Joshua had experienced up to this point. Scripture bestows this name upon one who was facing the "God Will Deliver" test, and passing it in spite of overwhelming odds.

Third, the new name revealed Joshua's destiny. It was a hint that God was going to use Joshua as a deliverer, not a self-appointed deliverer but one empowered by God. The fact that Moses, a prophet, initiated this change gave added might to the act. A person with prophetic insight was confirming Joshua's destiny and clarifying its nature.

Goodwin's expectancy principle was at work challenging the emerging leader.[13] The name change reflected Moses' expectations for his protege. Joshua, the potential national leader, would rise to the level of these expectations.

Process Item 11: Faith Challenge

In Numbers 13 and 14 Joshua accepted the challenge to spy out Canaan. God's promise of the Land had been given. Joshua chose to embrace a promise yet unfulfilled The challenge was to take steps of faith based on Yahweh's past promise and present command.

Throughout this incident, spiritual and ministerial formations were taking place preparing Joshua for what lay ahead. This challenge was a precursor to successive challenges that would occur throughout his ministry. He was learning to take calculated risks based on God's Word (Nu. 14:7,8), and discovering that divine affirmation would follow his steps of faith (14:30,38). God was also developing resilience and firmness of character.

In a negative light, Joshua saw how God dealt with those who failed a faith challenge (Nu. 14:40). The morning after their failure, the Israelites were ready to do what they should have done initially. However, it was too late (14:41-43). Joshua could see that timing was important. A challenge was to be met according to God's timetable. A life event was communicating a vital truth: those who reject faith challenges due to the risks involved, will not enter into the blessing associated with its success. What an important lesson for a military commander who would be in charge of developing strategies for upcoming battles.

13.See note nine.

Process Item 12: Prayer Power

As commander in battle with the Amalekites, Joshua learned a poignant lesson: the backbone of any work done for God is prayer (Ex. 17:8-16). While Joshua led the Israelite army, Moses lifted his hands heavenward in a prayer posture. Success was forthcoming as long as Moses kept his hands raised to the throne of the Lord (vv.11,16).

This incident speaks clearly. Victory is not due to military prowess, but to the power of God. Should Joshua want power in battle, he'd need power with God. Real power was not in the sword, but in the Lord.

This was a tremendous lesson to learn, and God saw fit to provide an early learning experience regarding it. Joshua had often witnessed Moses, the great prayer-power model, in spiritual action. Thus prayer's importance had frequently been impressed upon him. Now Joshua's success depended upon this spiritual exercise. Why? This budding leader needed to know that no one attains true spiritual leadership who thinks his/her power is his/her own, or that past successes are due to personal genius. When it would come time to take steps toward destiny fulfillment, when the Promised Land awaited conquest, the Israelites would be led by one who knew the power of prayer and was given to the exercise of the same.

Process Item 13: Networking Power

In Exodus 17:8-16 it's clear that Joshua was not fighting the battle against the Amalekites alone. Up on the hill was his mentor, Moses, and two other leaders who were used by God to channel power for Joshua (Collingridge 1987:35). This event, then, became an important lesson for Joshua. He learned that teamwork (interdependency) is necessary in spiritual leadership. Not all can pray effectively. Not all can fight effectively. Moses, Aaron, Hur, and Joshua were each necessary, in their unique contributions, to the successful outcome of the battle. Joshua was learning that relationships with other leaders are important. He probably sensed God's touch through this network of individuals.

Process Item 14: Isolation

Joshua accompanied Moses up the mountain of God (Ex. 24:9-18). For forty days and nights he was left alone as Moses responded to the Lord's call within the cloud.

During this time, Joshua was set aside from normal activity. He was alone, isolated from human involvement. His environment was free from many external influences and responsibilities. While isolation was not forced, Joshua's duties as an aide to Moses led him into this solitary position.

God frequently uses isolation to teach important lessons that could not be learned amidst the pressures of normal ministry (Clinton 1989:274). This seemed to be the case with Joshua. While he had been learning through Moses' example, it was time to gather a repertoire of his own experiences. God had just captured Joshua's attention through a visitation (Ex. 24:9,10). Now He was drawing him into a deeper relationship. Isolation was providing an opportunity to reflect on the God he had just seen. The recent glimpse of Yahweh must have stirred a spiritual hunger within Joshua. His focus was sharply turning toward God. He needed to learn that his first ministry was to the Lord.[14] Out of the strength of this ministry would flow divine life and effective ministry to others. This was an opportunity for divine encounter and impartation of heavenly vision. It was a chance to gain new perspective, rekindle a sense of destiny, and grow in prayer. God was processing His future leader in isolation.

Process Item 15: Divine Affirmation

In the midst of leadership backlash, Joshua received affirmation through a prophetic word (Nu. 14:30,38). The general populace had rejected Joshua's and Caleb's claims concerning the Land. The people were so angry that they were ready to stone their leaders (Nu.14:10). At this point, God's glory appeared. God pronounced judgment on the Israelites, but blessing upon Joshua and Caleb. He said, "Not one of you will enter the land...except Caleb son of Jephunneh and Joshua son of Nun" (Nu. 14:30).

Assurance of divine acceptance came in the midst of overwhelming rejection. When nearly everyone was against him, God met Joshua with acceptance. In doing this, the Lord was ministering personally to him, as well as making a public statement of affirmation. In essence the divine communication was, "Well done, good and faithful servant. "

Process Item 16: Mentoring

Joshua experienced ongoing mentoring by Moses. He shared the great leader's learning experiences (tandem training). Close association and observation of the elder leader enabled him to emulate what he saw (imitation modelling). Tandem training and imitation modelling helped transition him into responsible leadership. At Rephidim (Ex. 17:8-16) and in spying out the land (Nu. 13,14) Moses provided Joshua with opportunities to accept responsibility and control of a leadership function, role and task. Leadership release was taking place. The emerging leader was being prepared for the upcoming transition into a primary leadership role.[15]

14.In her book, Ministerine to the Lord, Roxanne Brant emphasized this truth. She summed up a major ministry problem: "So often the Lord of the work suffers while we are busy with the work of the Lord." Her book is a refreshing look at this primary ministry theme.

15.The success of a leadership transition "varies with respect to where the [emerging] leader had just been before" (Hollander 1978:60). Ministry tasks and visibility were helping Joshua move to a place of credibility prior to his placement as Moses' successor.

The two tasks Moses had given Joshua carried significant responsibility. It's likely that Moses was testing Joshua's faithfulness, skills and abilities. In other instances, Moses included Joshua in his spiritual experiences. Joshua had firsthand access to his mentor's personal times with the Lord. Moses took him into the holy of holies, into the tabernacle, and up the mountain (Ex. 24:9-18; 33:7-11). Other mentoring tactics included literary helps (Ex. 17:14 Josh 1:8) and informal instruction (Nu. 11:29-30). Thus, Joshua learned through modelling (Ex. 32:15-35), verbal instruction (Nu. 11:29-30), and the Book of the Law (Ex. 17: 18; Josh. 1:8).

A leadership philosophy evolved as Joshua's informal training progressed. He must have accumulated many leadership principles by adopting Moses' perspective. In spite of the differences in leadership style, similarities between Moses and Joshua indicate that many of these principles were internalized by Joshua as he matured.[16]

Sub-Phase C: Succession Confirmation

This period of time was initiated by God's selection of Joshua as Moses' successor (Nu. 27:12-23). It was marked by events confirming God's choice. It was a transitional segment in which Joshua moved into primary leadership position. Revelation was the catalyst. God revealed that Joshua was Moses' successor. Confirmation followed with public acknowledgment, affirmation, and commissioning. Final release into leadership took place with the death of Moses. Thus, the actual transition into position occurred.

The major process items in this sub-phase include the following:

1. Leadership Commital	5. Faith Challenge
2. Ministry Structural Insight	6. Destiny Revelation
3. Spiritual Authority Discovery	7. Double Confirmation
4. Word Item	8. Mentoring

Process Item 1: Leadership Committal

Joshua was commissioned to succeed Moses (Nu. 27:12-23: Deut. 31). The events portrayed in Numbers and Deuteronomy culminated in Joshua's public acceptance of God's leadership design for him. His selection and commissioning was thus accompanied by leadership commitment, a willingness to be used in God's service.

While evidence indicates that Joshua had been previously committed to serving Yahweh, these moments called for commitment renewal, and con-

---

16.See Appendix C for comparisons between Moses and Joshua.

scious decision to follow God into greater levels of responsibility. This was a pivotal point. Leadership commitment was the pivotal factor. From this time on, Joshua's life would have a new distinct flavor. Possibly for the first time, he and all of Israel clearly saw the roles and assignments God had for him/ The many formerof divine intent merged together to form a clear picture. Joshua was Moses' successor, the one who would lead God's people into the Promised Land. Leadership commitment was the first step into this new arena.

This pivotal point was a benchmark, or faith anchor, for days ahead. This benchmark, or faith anchor, for days ahead. This benchmark would be especially important since Joshua was stepping into the shoes of a spiritual giant. In days ahead, he could look back to this point with assurance that God had called him.

Process Item 2: Ministry Structural Insight

In the sucession selection passage (Nu. 27:12-23), Moses' prayer and prophetic word provided organizational insights. Limited structures were outlined, giving Joshua a general framework through which he could function and fulfill his calling. The first insight involved the structure of his leadership role. In prayer, Moses requested a successor who would lead the people out and bring them in, one who would be like a shepherd (v.17a). The second insight involved the governing structure. Eleazar was to be installed in a governing role in regard to the decision making process (v.21a). Moses was putting the leadership of Israel into both of their hands (although Joshua was assigned the primary role). God made it clear that there was to be a union between Joshua, the civil leader, and Eleazar, the spiritual leader.[17] They would need to work together (Collinridge 1987:49). The third insight involved ministry fuction. Joshua was called to take command of the Israelites' activities (v.21b). "At his command...the Israelites will go out, and ...come in." His leadership was to be structured so as to effectively implement the movement of the entire community. This would be no small task as he was dealing with an entire nation.[18]

Process Item 3: Spiritual Authority Discovery

At the time of Joshua's selection, God told Moses to give some of his authority to Joshua (Nu. 27:20). This authority probably involved both legiti-

---

17. The inclusion of Eleazar's spiritual leadership helped to cover any possible weaknesses in Joshua's ability to lead spiritually. It's also possible that Moses intended to provide a framework for godly counsel (cf. Prov. 15:22), or to set in place a check and balance on the abuse of power (cf. Hollander 1978:85). It should also be noted that later in Joshua's life, mature spiritual qualities were evident (cf. Josh. 3:7-8, 4:22-24, 5:13-6:5; 6:10; 7:10-13; 8:18,30-35).

18.Joshua probably did have some experience in orchestrating the movement of a large body of people, depending upon his involvement in the Israelites' exodus from Egypt and their migrations in the wilderness.

mate and spiritual authority.[19] Both of these authority types can be bestowed: the first through the granting of an office; the second through divine impartation. The office to which Joshua was being commissioned carried its own authority. The role itself produced common expectations for the followers and the leader. These expectations allowed Joshua to be a power holder, and anticipated the willing compliance of his followers.[20] Spiritual authority was imparted through the prophetic word (w.18-21) and laying on of hands (v.23; Deut 34:9). From a scriptural perspective, God imparts supernatural ability, grace and anointing in this way (Gen. 48:14-16; I Tim. 14:14 2 on. 1:6), Thus, this experience represents an advancement in the development of Joshua's authority. God was weaving a tight braid of authority which would be the core of Joshua's power in leadership.

Process Item 4: Word Item

The selection and commissioning accounts conveyed important words from the Lord which affected Joshua's committal, guidance, decision making, and spiritual authority. The first account in Numbers 27:12-23 contained a directional, prophetic word. God gave ministry insight and direction (vv.19-21a), along with a glimpse of future leadership (v.2lb). The second account in Deuteronomy 31 offered encouraging and prophetic words (vv.7,8,23). Twice God assured Joshua of His presence and told him to be strong and courageous. Twice God revealed Joshua's upcoming assignments. All of these communications built spiritual authority and guided Joshua into the harbor of God's plan. They would become a plumbline for future decision making. They were signposts along the journey of faith, marking his way.

Process Item 5: Faith Challenge

Joshua was confronted with two faith challenges. In the first instance he was challenged to take a step of faith toward God's promise (Deut. 31). God told him that he would lead Israel into the Land (v.7cf). He had revelation of God's intent and knew that he was being called upon to act on this basis. This meant embracing the divine call, an act he willingly performed (v.14).

The second challenge was recorded in Deuteronomy 34. It related to Joshua's succession of Moses, the unsurpassed leader. The Bible afforded

---

19.Hollander shares some insights on legitimate authority. He states, "Authority requires that a leader have a legitimate basis. Legitimacy may come from appointment, election, or from the willing support of followers. It is the basis for the acceptance of the leader's assemom of influence" (1978:66). Moses was giving Joshua this legitimacy in the commissioning act.

20.In a leader/follower relationship clear role understanding has a positive effect. T. O. Jacobs summed up this effect in his book, *Leadership and Exchange In Formal Organizations*:

> Where mutual expectations for what is necessary or desired can be developed, one membet of a relationship can then initiate action in conformity with the expectations of the other without causing the other to incur a post" (1970:340).

Moses an honorary position. "No prophet has arisen in Israel like Moses.... For no one has ever shown the mighty power or performed the awesome deeds that..." he did (v.12). It was challenging to step into the track laid by Moses and to carry on the leadership task he so adequately performed. However, in spite of his mentor's looming shadow, Joshua ascended the steps of faith to national leadership. He did this in compliance to Yahweh's revelation. His faith steps were met by divine affirmation (Josh. 1), and eventually ministry achievement (Josh. 5:33-12:24).

Process Item 6: Destiny Revelation

God revealed Joshua's destiny through succession selection (Nu. 27:12-23), commissioning (Deut. 31), and prophetic words (Deut. 3:21-29). This series of confirmations clinched Joshua's succession to the board of reality. God was making a plain statement of His intentions for Joshua, and taking steps toward realizing these intentions. Destiny fulfillment was on the horizon.

This sub-phase was a boundary time. Joshua was on the brink of destiny fulfillment. Change was rapidly moving him ahead. Destiny revelation kept this forward movement in pace. The momentum was powered by revelatory words and acts, such as the commissioning. Personal and public confirmation was the result. Corporate and individual directions were being clarified. God was establishing His leader both privately and in the eyes of the people.

Process Item 7: Double Confirmation

God commissioned Joshua and said, "Be strong and courageous, for you will bring the Israelites into the land I promised them on oath, and I myself will be with you" (Deut. 31:23). Up to this point, there had been formal delivery of Moses' authority to Joshua (Nu. 27:20). Now, however, Joshua received confirmation of this authority from God Himself (Collingridge 1987:52). God told Joshua, "I will be with you!" The new leader personally heard from the Lord regarding his appointment.

Process Item 8: Mentoring

Skillful mentoring was crucial at this time. It was a season of leadership transition, and success would depend on Moses' ability to pass the baton gracefully. He carefully installed his protege into office (Nu. 27:18-23), and gave final instructions and encouragement (Deut. 31). As his last mentoring act, Moses passed the national leadership on to Joshua. (For more details regarding this transition see the comments in the conclusion.)

Chart 5—Table of Principles-Phase II

Name	Observation	Principles
Affirmation	1. Joshua received many affirmations from the Lord; some of them were public.	1a. God will give a leader appropriate affirmations. 1b. All leaders need affimation from time to time. 1c. God will confirm and vindicate leaders who follow Him. 1d. When necessary, God will publicly affirm His leaders.
Authority	1. At Rephidim, Joshua was submitted to Moses (Ex. 17:8-16). 2. Aaron and Hur supported Moses' uplifted hands (Ex. 17:12). 3. Joshua witnessed Moses' direct and forceful use of authority in Exodus 32:15-35. 4. Aaron tried to shift blame for failure on the people (Ex. 32:15-35). 5. Moses exercised his authority swiftly in Ex. 32:26-29. 6. Moses required the people to identify who's side they were on (Ex. 32:26).	1a. Those in authority must be under authority. 2a. Those at the highest level of authority need the support of others. 3a. The exercise of forceful, direct authority can be appropriate in times of crisis. 4a. Authority is willing to take responsibility. 4b. Authority does not "pass the buck." 5a. Authority is not afraid to act. 6a. A crisis event may require a leader to identify committed followers and seek an outward show of that committment.
Conflict/Crisis	1. Conflict and crisis marked Israel's departure from Egypt (Ex. 7-14). 2. God led the Israelites out of Egypt, across the Red Sea, and into the wilderness. 3. During a crisis, Joshua experienced a public display of God's glory (Nu. 14:10). 4. Joshua and Moses faced a major crisis after a significant spiritual experience (Ex. 33:15-35).	1a. A high pressure atmosphere can create the internal and external pressure necessary to advance a person, or group, in God's plan. 2a. God will guide His people through crisis. 2b. An ability to discern God's guidance is crucial in times of crisis. 3a. God will publicly vindicate His leaders who are in right relationship with Him. 4a. Spiritual experiences don't immunize one from the difficulties of life. 4b. A spiritual experience will often be tested on the crucible of crisis.
Destiny Fulfillment	1. At the Red Sea, God revealed Himself as "the Lord who fights against Egypt" (Ex. 14:25). 2. Joshua experienced the promised exodus from Egypt, an event foretold hundreds of years earlier. 3. Joshua's birth name, Oshea (deliverer), was changed to Jehoshua (God will deliver).	1a. God will reveal Himself in the way(s) necessary to move a person, or group, into destiny fulfillment. 2a. God will fulfill His promises, though there may be an extended delay (cf. Hab. 2:3). 3a. A name can be a significant item pointing toward one's destiny.
Faith Challenge	1. Joshua embraced God's challenge to enter the land in spite of visible evidence to the contrary (Nu. 13:28, 29). There were repercussions. 2. The children of Israel rejected God's challenge to enter the Land. When later they decided to obey, God did not support their efforts (Nu. 14:40). 3. God affirmed Joshua in this challenge, but judged the Israelites (Nu. 14:35-38).	1a. Steps of faith must be taken on the basis of God's word and not circumstances. 1b. Accomplishments for God will often involve risks. 2a. Faith challenges have an intervention time associated with them. 2b. If the intervention time is missed, God removes His backing from the venture. 2c. Those who reject a faith challenge due to the risks involved, will not enter into the blessing associated with its success. 3a. God will affirm steps of faith taken in obedience to Him. 3b. Those who accept faith challenges will receive the promise and be rewarded. 3c. A challenge, rightly handled, affirms a leader in his/her role (Collingridge, 1987:65).
Isolation	1. Joshua was alone on the mountain of God for forty days and nights waiting for Moses (Ex. 24:18).	1a. There are times when leaders will experience isolation in the course of fulfilling their duties.
Leadership Lessons	1. Joshua expeienced Yahweh as a God of war in the Exodus, at Rephidim (Ex. 17:8-16), and in an encounter with the Lord of Hosts (Josh. 5:13-6:5). 2. These experiences prepared Joshua for the conquest of Canaan.	1a. God will repeat important leadership lessons until they are understood. 2a. God's revelations to a leader will reflect the task(s) he/she has been called to do.
Leadership Selection	1. Moses praved for a successor (Nu. 27:15-17). 2. Moses was mery specific in his prayer for a successor (Nu. 27:17). 3. God chose Joshua (Nu. 27:18). 4. Joshua was "a man in whom is the Spirit" (Nu. 27:18). 5. God gave Joshua double confirmation regarding his appointment as Moses' successor (Deut. 31:23).	1a. A leader must depend upon God, in prayer, when choosing a successor. 2a. A leader should be specific in his/her prayers about a successor. 3a. God always has someone prepared to lead His people. 3b. Leadership, if it is real, is from God. 3d. God will make his leadership selection clear to the person responsible for that choice. 4a. An important selection criterion is that the selected leader must be filled with God's Spirit (cf. Acts 6:2-4). 4b. True spiritual leadership emanates from God's Spirit (Collingridge, 1987:62). 5a. God will confirm His appointment to the chosen leader. 5b. In a major decision like leadership selection, the matter should be "established by the testimony of two or three witnesses" (2 Cor. 13:1).

Chart 5—Table of Principles-Phase II cont.

Name	Observation	Principles
Leadership Transition	1. Moses prayed for a successor (Nu. 27:17).	1a. Leadership transition must begin with prayer. 1b. Leadership transition should be carried out in the cradle of prayer (Collingridge, 1987:64).
	2. God told Moses to lay his hands on Joshua (Nu. 27:20).	2a. Gifts, authority, and power can be transferred by the laying on of hands (cf. Gen. 48:14-16; 1 Tim. 14:14; 2 Tim. 1:6).
	3. All of this was done before the congregation (Nu. 27:19).	3a. Effective leadership transition will involve a public act acknowledging this transition. 3b. By publicly anointing a new leader, the former leader symbolically shifts leadership authority to the successor. 3c. The public act confirms and establishes the new leader in the eyes of the people.
	4. God told Moses to place Joshua before Eleazar (Nu. 27:19).	4a. Spiritual leaders should be involved in the selection of new leaders (Collingridge, 1987:64). 4b. Public religious approval helps the transition.
	5. Moses was to give Joshea some of his authority (Nu. 27:20).	5a. Authority can be imparted. 5b. The impartation of authority will give the new leader status in the eyes of the people. 5c. The endorsement of the old leader will help establish the new leader in his/her role. 5d. In successful leadership transition, there may be a period of time in which the old regime shares authority with the new, thus easing ghe transition. 5e. During a transition in which responsibility is being gradually shifted to another, authority must also be granted.
	6. Moses installed Eleazar the assist in the decision-making process (Nu. 27:21).	6a. In a transition, it is important to establish a structure which will strengthen and enhance the new leader's role. 6b. When transferring leadership, the senior leader should be aware of potential weaknesses in the new leader, and recruit individuals with complementary skills.
	7. The general duties of Joshua and Eleazar were outlined (Nu. 27:17, 20, 21).	7a. New roles should be delineated to avoid confusion and conflict after the former leader has left.
	8. During the period of transition, Joshua received a word from the Lord (Deut. 31:8, 23).	8a. A word from the Lord will help guide a leader through leadership transition. 8b. A word from the Lord will give personal and/or public confirmation of the leadership selection. 8c. Words from the Lord serve as personal/public plumblines during times of change. 8d. Spiritual sensitivity is necessary in successful leadership transition.
	9. In a public address, Moses affirmed Joshua and the call upon his life (Deut. 3:21-29).	9a. The departing leader can do much to bolster the new leader in the eyes of the people. 9b. The departing leader can instill, in his followers, confidence in their new leader.
	10. Joshua wsa called to succeed an incomparable leader, Moses (Deut. 34:10-12).	10a. A leader, no matter how gifted, is never indispensable. 10b. God will always raise up someone to step into a leadership position. 10c. The success and giftedness of yesterday's leaders must not hinder today's leaders from forging ahead with the resources available to them.
	1. Moses gave Joshua important written material (Ex. 17:14; Josh. 1:8).	1a. A leader should keep a written record of what God has done for him/her (Collingridge, 1987:56). 1b. A person preparing for leadership will benefit by reading the writings of other leaders .
	1. The Passover and Sabbath rites initiated during Joshua's time. Manna samples were also preserved as memorials. They were to be kept as reminders of what God had done.	1a. Rites serve as memorials of God's acts. 1b. Memorials testify to what God has done, can do, and will do. 1c. Memorials communicate a concern for the preservation and transmission of truth. 1d. A leader, seeing beyond present ministry impact, will understand the importance of establishing memorials.
	2. Moses left significant writings for Joshua (Ex. 17:14; Josh 1:8).	2a. Literary works can serve as memorials to God's acts. 2b. Leaders need to establish memorials for subsequent generations.

Chart 5—Table of Principles-Phase II cont.

Name	Observation	Principles
Shared Leadership	1. The victory at Rephidim was won by a conglomerate effort (Ex. 17:8-16). 2. Moses welcomed Eldad and Medad's spiritual input (Nu. 11:24-30). 3. Moses installed Eleazar alongside Joshua to assist in Joshua's new leadership role (Nu. 27:18-21).	1a. Teamwork (interdependency) is necessary in spiritual leadership (cf. 1 Cor. 3:5). 1b. Leaders must learn to support each facet of the work (Collingridge, 1987:54). 1c. Good leaders must relate to other leaders (Collingridge, 1987:63). 2a. True spiritual leadership welcomes the giftedness of others. 2b. It is lonely at the top. God's answer to this is a shared spirit with other leaders. 2c. Good leaders are thakful when others exercise their gifts. 2d. A good leader will endeavor to find others who can share the load with him/her. 2e. A leader should not feel threatened by another's ministry (Collingridge, 1987:59). 3a. A leader should gather other gifted leaders to fill in the giftedness/ability gap. 3b. Civil leaders should seek advice from religious leaders (Collingridge, 1987:58).
Spirituality	1. In Exodus 33:11, Joshua spent time alone with God in the Tent of Meeting. (See also Ex. 24:18-21).	1a. A love for the intimate presence of God is requisite for spiritual leadership and authority. 1b. A personal encounter with God is more valuable to the development of a leader than vicarious knowledge. 1c. A person aspiring to leadership must desire a greater vision of God (Collingridge, 1987:57). 1d. Personal encounters with God help growing leaders take their eyes off human leaders (Collingridge, 1987:57). 1e. A leader must be aware of God:s intimate presence. 1f. A potential leader should demonstrate a hunger for more of God. 1g. True spiritual leadership demands a love for time alone with God (Collingridge, 1987:58). 1h. A good leader will be a prayer example (Collingridge, 1987:58).
Testing	1. The people wanted to stone Joshua (Nu. 14). While he had observed this type of reaction toward Moses, this was the first time he experienced a direct threat against himself. 2. The testing at Meribah resulted in a major conflict and a serious spiritual problem (Ex. 17:1-7). 3. Because of majority unbelief, Joshua faced forty years in the wilderness (Nu. 14). 4. The people wanted to stone Joshua (Nu. 14).	1a. Times of testing will help one assimilate lessons learned by past observations. 1b. Life's tests will give opportunity for sifting through principles learned by osmosis. 2a. A wrong response, left unchecked among followers, can become a point of major conflict and a serious spiritual problem. 3a. A leader may face difficulties because of others' wrong choices (Collingridge, 1987:61). 3b. Unbelief among follower can result in negative repercussions for leaders (Collingridge, 1987:61). 4a. There are times when a leader will have to stand against the rage of followers. 4b. When people reject a leaders, they are actually rejecting God (cf. Matt. 10:41-42).

Chart 6   LSP Overview and Detailed Phase Chart III

	A. Entering the Land (Joshua 1-5:12)	B. Possessing the Land (Joshua 5:13-12:24)	C. Establishing the Land (Joshua 13-22)	D. Retaining the Land (Joshua 23,24)
Development Sub-Phase	A. Entering the Land (Joshua 1-5:12)	B. Possessing the Land (Joshua 5:13-12:24)	C. Establishing the Land (Joshua 13-22)	D. Retaining the Land (Joshua 23,24)
Essential Geography	Jordan River/Canaan	Canaan	Canaan	Canaan
Context/Events/People	Joshua Assumes National Leadership/Crossing into the Promised Land	Battles to Possess the Land and Related Items	Land Division Among the Israelites/A New Society Established	Period of Afterglow for Joshua/Joshua's Two Final Speeches
Major Process Factors/Detailed Items	FOUNDATIONAL (TRANSITIONAL) • Obedience Check MINISTRY (EXPANSION) • Word Item • Literary Item • Faith Challenge • Destiny Revelation GUIDANCE • Divine Affirmation • Destiny Fulfillment	MINISTRY (FOUNDATIONAL) • Relationship Insight MINISTRY (TRANSITIONAL) • Word Check MINISTRY (EXPANSION) • Spiritual Authority Discovery • Word Item • Literary Item • Destiny Revelation • Faith Challenge • Prayer Challenge • Power Item • Prayer Power • Crisis UNIQUE MINISTRY (GUIDANCE) • Divine Affirmation • Ministry Affirmation • Flesh Act • Destiny Fulfillment	UNIQUE MINISTRY (MATURING) • Ideal Role Discovery • Influence Mix Discovery UNIQUE MINISTRY (GUIDANCE) • Destiny Fulfillment	UNIQUE MINISTRY (GUIDANCE) • Destiny Fulfillment
Roles	Military National Leader	Military National Leader	Military Leader/Administrator/Statesman	Spiritual Advisor
Sphere of Influence	Direct Local/National	Direct Local/National Large Organizational Indirect International	Direct Local/National Large Organizational Indirect International	Direct National Indirect National/International

NARRATIVE EXPLANATION OF PHASE III
FULFILLING A DESTINY -
THE CONQUEST AND ESTABLISHMENT OF CANAAN

Overview

Under the auspice of Moses, Joshua had been trained and commissioned as Israel's national leader. Now, without a mentor, Joshua was to take a firm grip on the leadership reigns. With years of preparation behind him, he stepped onto the stage of destiny fulfillment. With a clear-cut assignment and firmly established direction, he set out to lead the people of Israel toward accomplishment of their corporate goal.

In this phase, there were four distinct movements aimed at reaching this goal (promise fulfillment). These movements include the following sub-phases:[21]

A. Entering the Land (Josh. 1-5:12)

B. Possessing the Land (Josh. 5:13-2:24)

C. Establishing the Land (Josh. 13-22)

D. Retaining the Land (Josh. 23,24)

Each of these sub-phases represent short-term tasks aimed at attaining the long-range goal, life in the land. The first sub-phase, Entering the Land, was transitional both for Joshua and the Israelites. The events occurring during this time dramatically marked the beginning of a new era. Entrance into the land signified a new place. Circumcision spoke of a new spirituality. The ceasing of wilderness food (manna) pointed toward a new life and economy (Hamlin 1983:38,39). And the manifestation of a long-awaited promise (500-600 years) proclaimed a unique moment in destiny fulfillment. The emphasis in the sec-

---

21.The idea for these divisions came from Davis' treatment of the text in his book, No Falling Words (1988).

ond sub-phase, Possessing the Land, was on conquest, or land acquisition through military struggle. The thrust was acquisition of the promise. The third sub-phase, Establishing the Land, highlighted Israel's settlement in the acquired land. While land acquisition would still take place, the important elements included land distribution and the establishment of a holy society therein. The final sub-phase in Joshua's life was Retaining the Land. This was a time of afterglow in which his influence was exerted for the benefit of future national life. He was planning for life after his death. Joshua's concern centered on maintaining a holy society in the Land. He led his people into destiny fulfillment (Sub-Phase A), into partial possession of that destiny (Sub-Phase B), into a life established in that destiny (Sub-Phase C), and into truth that would ensure the ongoing experience of that destiny (Sub-Phase D). The final sub-phase was a boundary time, marking the end of his leadership and pointing toward Israel's future.

Sub-Phase A: Entering the Land

Entering the Land was a brief transitional period marked by Joshua's leadership of Israel into Canaan. It was initiated by Moses' death (Deut. 34; Josh. 1:2) and completed after preparatory steps for war were taken. These steps included Israel's strategic (Josh.2), physical (Josh. 3), and spiritual (Josh 4-5:12) positioning. As Joshua led the Israelites through this process his leadership was established (Josh. 1:5b;4:14). A positive response to tests indicated his readiness for conquest (Josh. 4-5:12). The end of this period was symbolically celebrated by the sudden ceasing of manna food (Josh. 5:12).[22]

The key process items in this sub-phase include the following:

1. Obedience Check   5. Faith Challenge
2. Word Item   6. Destiny Revelation/Confirmation
3. Literary Item   7. Divine Affirmation
4. Spiritual Authority Discovery   8. Destiny Fulfillment

Process Item I: Obedience Check

Joshua and the Israelites had just made tremendous commitments to God and to one another (Josh. 1). They were eager to take the land. But before they could their commitments were to be tested by the Lord.

Before conquest could begin, the new leader needed to test his mettle without mentoring support. Would Joshua follow the Lord along the divinely prescribed path, or, as the new leader, would he assume his own direction? It was one thing to hear and obey Moses, and quite another to perceive God's voice

---

22. For the first time in forty years the manna from heaven ceased and the Isaelites began to eat the produce of Canaan (Ex. 16:34,35).

and walk in obedience. With Moses gone, would Joshua even be able to hear from God? If so, would he transfer his faithful obedience to the Lord? To answer these questions, obedience tests (and faith challenges) were necessary.

God was also testing the Israelites' commitment. They had professed unfeigned obedience to Joshua (Josh. 1:16-18). Would they follow through, or would they rebel against Joshua as their ancestors had rebelled against Moses?

This sub-phase ends with two obedience checks (Josh. 4,5). These checks were instrumental in testing Joshua and the Israelites, and in moving them into spiritual readiness necessary for conquest. Both Joshua and the Israelites responded positively to this processing, and moved into the next phase of God's plan.

In the first obedience check God told Joshua to establish a stone memorial (Josh. 4). God said, "Choose twelve men from among the people, one from each tribe, and tell them to take up twelve stones from the middle of the Jordan from right where the priests stood and carry them over with you and put them down at the place where you stay tonight" (vv.2,3). If, as it appears, this was the totality of God's command, then Joshua not only heard and obeyed God's direction, but he also understood its significance. He knew that the stones were to serve as signs, or memorials, of what God had done at the Jordan (vv.5-7, 21-24). Thus, Joshua's obedience was full. Not only had he obeyed the direct command, but he also perceived God's underlying purpose and communicated it to the people. In this way, he secured their conformity. Joshua and the Israelites obeyed God in this seemingly minor, and yet necessary act. As a result, God exalted Joshua in the sight of all Israel (v.14).

While God may require a leader's unqualified obedience, a mark of mature leadership is discernment of God's intent as well as His direction. A leader is wise not to require blind obedience. Perceiving and communicating the reason for a particular course of action can do much to encourage the willful compliance of followers.[23]

The second instance involved the circumcision at Gilgal (Josh. 5:1-12). God told Joshua, "Make flint knives and circumcise the Israelites again" (v.12). This was the necessary, final step preceding aggressive movement into Canaan. Apparently these Israelites had not been introduced to the underlying structure of their parent's corporate existence (v.7) (Hamlin 1983:32). Through circumcision this introduction took place. The people remained in the camp until they were "healed" (v.8). In the Hebrew "healed" has two meanings: to be "healed from the wound" and to he "restored to life" (Hamlin 1983:34). Not only were the people being healed from the physical effects of circumcision,

---

23. A follower acts within the features of a "situation which he or she sees as major, and these are usually defined by leaders. In determining 'the way things are.' the individual relies upon other people's view of reality, especially the leader's" (Hollander 1978:14).

they were also being restored to life as a result of this act. Circumcision marked a time of restoration to spiritual wholeness (v.9). Thus Joshua's obedience was crucial. Only through sensitive obedience, one step at a time, would he be able to lead his people into destiny fulfillment.

Process Item 2: Word Item

During this sub-phase there were at least two word items (Josh. 1:2-9; 3:7,8). The first was instrumental in transitioning Joshua into promise fulfillment (Josh. 1:1-9). It provided goals and direction (vv.2,8), promise (vv.3,5,6c,9), destiny revelation (vv.4,6b), and strong encouragement (vv. 6,7,9). All of these elements were necessary to thrust Joshua into his new role. As a result of this word he began to act (1:10 2:1). He organized the people. The people followed his lead and gave him their full commitment (w.16-18).[24] God's immediate goals were clear(w.2,6,8).[25]   And important theological truths were communicated (e.g., "I will never leave you"; "obey all the law...that you may be successful3. The result was a forward movement of faith which would carry Joshua and the Israelites through this sub-phase into conquest.[26]

Sometimes giant steps are required to move into destiny fulfillment creating a need for a strong catalyst and high levels of momentum. Such seemed to be the case in Joshua's situation. God's word was this catalyst and source of forward movement. A spark ignited and Joshua began to act. A momentum was triggered which climaxed in a majestic entrance into the Promised Land.

The second word (Josh. 3:7-8) added fuel to the momentum begun in chapter one. God promised to exalt His leader, gave brief directions concerning the crossing of the Jordan, and challenged Joshua to continue in his steps of faith. In the first part of the divine communique God promised to exalt Joshua. The Great Psychologist was preparing him for the next step. This affirmation was followed by a seemingly ridiculous command. Joshua was to instruct the priests to stand in the river. Just in case this directive might snag him along the banks of unbelief all he needed to do was remember God's promise, "Today I will begin to exalt you."

24.Hollander makes an important observation. He refers to the leadership process as a "two-way influence relationship aimed primarily at attaining mutual goals." He concludes that leadership is not merely the task of the leader. Leadership requires the cooperation and efforts of followers (1978:2).

25."When goals are clear, and largely agreed to, the leader's job is made easier" (Hollander 1978: 15).

26.It was at this point, after God's Word had been received and preparation begun, that the Isaelites expressed united commitment to Joshua. Something happened that encouraged a united desire u, move forward. According to Hollander, when a leader can secure and maintain unity, "members are mofe likely to stick together and be involved in more favorable interactions." Also, they can "be engaged effectively in seeking common goals" (1978:90).

Process Item 3: Literary

As Joshua assumed leadership, God emphasized the importance of a book, the "Book of the Law" (Josh. 1:8). In fact, throughout the Book of Joshua the written Law of Moses was stressed, along with its importance in Israel's economy (cf. Josh. 8:32-35; 24:25-27) (Davis 1969:31). In each of these contexts, Law (Torah) meant guidance, instruction, and teaching. It could best be translated "God's Teaching" Hamlin 1983:6). This body of literature, God's Teaching, carried with it full divine authority. As such, it would be vital in determining the success or failure of Joshua's leadership. Not only was he required to know the law, he was also told to meditate therein.[27] Why? Because constant, careful interaction with this book (God's Word) would prove to be his power for obedience, an obedience necessary for obtaining God's promises. God would use this book, time and again, to guide and instruct him along the pathway of service. It was his key to continued life and leadership. So valuable was it that Joshua later bequeathed it as a living legacy to God's people for their continued journey of faith (Josh. 22:5 23:6).

Process Item 4: Spiritual Authority Discovery

God strengthened Joshua's spiritual authority early in his new role. This was necessary to graft him into a high profile position. While Joshua had gained legitimate authority (Nu. 27:18-23 Josh. 1:1-9), and had exercised a measure of competent authority (Josh. 2), now he was discovering a new dimension in spiritual authority (Josh. 3).

Obedience to God's word (Josh. 3:7,8) led to a demonstration of divine power (Josh. 3:15,16). This supernatural act validated Joshua's leadership. Spiritual authority was growing for two reasons. First, Joshua was experiencing God in a new dimension. Never had a demonstration of power accompanied his leadership acts in this way. The people saw God move and recognized the divine hand on his life. Second, Joshua was functioning much like his former mentor. The authority that rested on Moses was now on him. The God who moved dramatically on Moses' behalf was working with Joshua. The people could look to him just as they had to Moses. Moses was gone, but in Joshua they would find a man with a similar anointing.[28]

Immediately after crossing the Jordan memorials were established at Yahweh's behest (Josh. 4). Not only did these memorials serve as reminders of

---

27.God told Joshua not to let this Book of the Law depart from his mouth (Josh. 1:8a). Having God's teaching in his mouth related to two things. First, the mouth is for eating. The Book of the Law was to be "digested" so that it would become part of his life. Second, the mouth is for speaking. Joshua would be responsible for communicating God's word to others (cf. Josh. 8:30-3R 24) (Hamlin 1983:6).

28.This is a positive result of mentoring influence, and is quite helpful especially when the former leader had a high level of respect and influence among the people.

God's deliverance, they also engendered a faith-filled awe in their leader. Not only did they proclaim God's acts, they also announced a leader's success and courageous faith.

The Israelites saw God's power (Josh. 3) and wisdom (Josh. 4) at work through Joshua's life, but they weren't the only ones. The surrounding nations would soon hear of the Jordan River event and see the mighty stones. Already the fear of Israel had fallen on a nearby city (Josh. 2:24). Spiritual authority was developing. God was expanding Joshua's power base. His influence was increasing among the Israelites and moving into the surrounding nations.

Process Item 5: Faith Challenge

Joshua was commissioned to lead the Israelites into their inheritance. In order to do this, he had to take three significant steps of faith: preparation for entering the land (Josh. 1:10-18); spying out the land (Josh. 2); and crossing the Jordan (Josh. 3).[29] These incidents represent successive challenges based on God's revelation in Joshua 1:1-9. Had Joshua stopped at any point, he would not have moved through this passage into destiny fulfillment. Great steps of faith are required to step into a great destiny.[30]

Joshua responded to God's challenge (Josh. 1:1-9) by ordering the officers to prepare the people to cross the Jordan (1:10). 'The immediate challenge facing Joshua was the organization of the tribes and preparation of food for the journey to Canaan" (Davis 1969:32). This was not something new for Joshua. He had probably learned much about mass movement in the Exodus. However, in "any challenging venture, the first step is always the hardest" (Hughes 1987:25). But Joshua boldly proceeded, supporting his move with a visionary faith statement (ill). The people caught the vision (vv.16-18). And his step of faith was met with affirmation through their eager and supportive response.

However, in-house preparation was not enough (Josh. 2). True faith will take aggressive steps outside one's comfort zone. If Joshua believed God's

29.Some of the functions of leadership include organizing, directing, coordinating efforts, defining the situation, setting goals, and maintaining the group (Hollander 1978:3). In the st four chapters of the Book of Joshua, Joshua was involved in each of these functions. Joshua organized the preparations for entrance into Canaan (Josh. 110,11). He directed and coordinated these efforts (Josh. 190;2:1W6:13). The situation was defined when he outlined the steps to be taken for crossing the river (Josh. 3:9-13). A three day goal had been set for the accomplishment of this task (Josh. 191). And a memorial of stone was erected for the purpose of maintaining the group distinctive as the people of God (Josh. 4:20-24).

30.Ihe first four chapters of Joshua can alternately be viewed as one faith challenge. When viewed this way the steps of the challenge include the following: a word from the Lord that challenges (Josh. t2); divine affirmation (:Josh. 2:9-11,24); a time of realizing the impossible nature of what needs to be done (Josh. 3:1); the central position of God (Josh. 3:2,3); divine affirmation following the initial steps of preparation (Josh. 3:7); a purification (Josh. 3:5); the initial faith step (Josh 3:15,16); an acknowledgment that God is at work (Josh. 3: 17); and the establishment of a memorial (Josh. 4)

word (Josh. 1:1-9), then the warrior had best take preliminary military action - spying out the land. This is what Joshua did. His action was met with affirmation (Josh. 2:9-11, 24).

Finally, God instructed Joshua to cross the Jordan River (Josh. 3). This event was a corporate milestone marking the transition into inheritance. It was a key moment in Joshua's leadership, but a moment fraught with challenge.

> It was a fearful order. The fifteenth verse of chapter 3 tells us that the Jordan was in flood stage.... For modern armies, such situations are difficult; for the Israelites, it was a physical impossibility. And God gave no hint of how to do it.
>
> Moreover, Joshua knew that crossing the Jordan meant throwing in the gauntlet. It was a declaration of war - a fight to the finish. Joshua knew that as soon as he crossed the Jordan, the enemies would assemble and fight with the tenacity of those fighting for home and hearth. All seven nations would muster their bravest forces. The giants of Anak would come running...To top it off, he was not taking a real, unified army into Canaan, but a mixed multitude of soldiers, as well as women and children whose fathers had proved unfaithful time and time again (Hughes 1987:2425).

The challenge was immense. Once Joshua led the Israelites across the Jordan there would be no retreat. Retreat would be cut off. Joshua would be committed. But it would be a commitment he would have to make, for full possession of God's promises requires ongoing steps of faith.

What was the purpose of this challenge? Joshua summed it up, "This is how you will know that the living God is among you and that he will certainly drive out before you the Canaanites, Hivites, Perizzites, Girgashites, Amorites and Jebusites" (Josh. 3:10).[31] In demonstrating His delivering power at the Jordan, God was providing a foundation for the reasoning of faith: "If Yahweh can tame a raging river, he can also repel attacking Amorites....If he can get you into the land, he can surely give you the land.. (Davis 1988:36). The Jordan crossing was to be a point of reference for Joshua's faith as he progressed into Canaan.

Process Item 6: Destiny Revelation/Confirmation

In Joshua 1:1-9 God revealed the scope and historical nature of Joshua's destiny. His future assignment was partially revealed when God told him, "I will give you every place where you set (*darak*) your foot" (v. 3). The word

---

31.This was the "reasoning of faith that Israel failed to use in Exodlls 16; they should have realized that the God who delivered them from Egypt (Exod. 14-15) would not let go of them in the wilderness" (Davis 1988:36).

darak symbolizes the "action, not of a conqueror, but of a tenant receiving the land as a gift" (Hamlin 1983:8). God had promised to give the Israelites the land of Canaan. Joshua's task was to receive that gift through conquest. A parallel verb, yararh, clarifies God's revelation to Joshua. It means the occupation and organization of a society according to God's teaching (Hamlin 1983:10). Not only was Joshua called to receive God's gift through conquest, he was also commissioned to occupy and organize a new, holy society in the land. The parameters of this society were then outlined (Josh. 1:4) and success assured (Josh.l:5). Then God told Joshua, "You will lead these people to inherit the land I swore to their forefathers to give them" (Josh. 1:6). God was revealing the historical nature of Joshua's destiny. His future was intricately linked to historical realities. It was anchored in past promises that had present and future implications. This leader was not an isolated individual, but a link in the network of God's timeless plan.

Process Item 7: Divine Affirmation

Because this sub-phase was a key to moving Joshua into destiny fulfillment, divine affirmations were abundant. Over and over again, God affirmed Joshua. Affirmations are particularly important during transition and when one's progress involves new and challenging events. Joshua was making his first decisions in a new role. Many changes were unraveling. Encouragement and ministry support were needed.

Affirmation came through a prophetic word (Josh. 1:1-9); the Israelites' willing commitment to followership (Josh. 1:16-18) a good report (Josh. 2:24); a power demonstration (Josh. 3:14-17); and a sovereign act of exaltation (Josh. 4:14). In these affirmations Joshua was assured of the continuity of God's promise, presence, word, people, and power. These stepping stones of continuity gave him stability during this transitional period into leadership.[32]

It's significant that these affirmations were preceded by God's statement, "Moses my servant is dead" (Josh. 1:2). Joshua would no longer have the wisdom and support of his former mentor, but he need not be discouraged or afraid. Though Moses was gone the ancient stepping stones were in place. For centuries they had upheld his forefathers on their journey of faith.

Process Item 8: Destiny Fulfillment

The crossing of the Jordan was a significant act in the fulfillment of God's promise to Joshua and the Israelites (Josh. 3). God's destiny promise to Joshua was summed up in Yahweh's word to Israel: "Not one of you will enter the land I swore with uplifted hand to make your home, except Caleb son of

---

32.Joshua's stability in his new role was affected by his past interactions with the people. These earlier interactions, guided and nurtured by Moses, must have created a sense of trust and ease among his followers

Jephunneh and Joshua son of Nun" (Nu. 14:30). Israel's magnificent entrance into the Promised Land was a promise realization, particularly for their leader. Joshua's destiny was not yet fully accomplished, but step-by-step, revelation was taking the shape of physical reality. A little at a time previous destiny processing was coming into completion.

Sub-Phase B: Possessing the Land

Possessing the Land focuses on Joshua's possession of Canaan. Joshua diligently tackled this task with tremendous leadership skill. His main role was that of military leader and strategist. He was able to draw from skills acquired during the foundational (Life In Egypt) and formational (Exodus and Wilderness) phases of his life.

This time frame represented a crisis mode (war) for both Joshua and the Israelites. Aspects of Joshua's character emerged in this atmosphere that were not evident at other times.[33] Previously, Moses had been the visionary and Joshua the administrator of that vision. While Joshua continued to administrate the details of his mentor's vision, a new dynamic was released. He displayed courage, aggressiveness, decisiveness, and visionary characteristics that weren't apparent in earlier or later stages. Possibly for the first time, he was seen as a leader in his own right.

Joshua's sphere of influence increased in depth and breadth.[34] Influence among the Israelites deepened through military successes and accompanying affirmations. Indirect influence expanded further into the international scene. Conquests, and news of conquest, impacted the surrounding Canaanite nations.

This segment of Joshua's life was initiated by a pivot-point event, an encounter with the commander of the Lord's army.[35] Here, Yahweh was established as conquest commander. This sub-phase ended after Joshua 12. A change was indicated by an indefinite passage of time and a different emphasis. The emphasis shifted to the establishment of the land.

33.The *Life Training* manual, a personality profile workbook, indicates that one's basic behavior orientation during favorable conditions can be different from behavior orientations during stress or conflict (Stuart Atkins, Inc., 1978).

34.According to Bobby, "Measures of influence include extensive (quantity), comprehensive (scope, areas of influence), and intensive (depth of influence in a given area. (Clinton 1989:230)

35.Other pivotal events in Joshua's life include the battle at Rephidim (Ex. 17:8-16), the spy mission u. 13,14), the Jordan River crossing (Josh. 3), the theophany (Josh. 4), and the incident with the Gibeonites (Josh. 9).

The major process items in this sub-phase include the following:

1. Relationship Insight
2. Word Check
3. Spiritual Authority Discovery
4. Word Item
5. Literary Item
6. Destiny Revelation
7. Faith Challenge

8. Prayer Challenge
9. Power Item
10. Prayer Power
11. Crisis
12. Divine Affirmation
13. Ministry Affirmation
14. Flesh Act
15. Destiny Fulfillment

Process Item I: Relationship Insight

Chapter seven of the Book of Joshua describes Israel's defeat by the small army at Ai. The reason for defeat was sin (vv. 1,21). Achan, a man of wealth, coveted and stole banned booty from Jericho. He thought "he was committing a hidden sin that even God did not see. He also thought that it would not hurt anyone else. But how pitifully wrong he was on both counts!" (Hughes 1987:85). His sin not only caused Israel's defeat and discouragement (vv.2-5), but also Joshua's despair (vv.6-9). It was not until sin was uncovered and punished, that God's wrath lifted (v.26).

What was Joshua learning through all of this? He was learning a difficult lesson regarding the solidarity of God's people. Although Achan committed the troublesome misdeed, scriptures testify that it was "the people of Israel who broke faith (7:1), sinned (v.ll), transgressed the covenant, took, stole, and lied (v.ll)" (Hamlin 1983:57-58). When one fails it effects the entire community. One person's sin can cause the defeat and destruction of God's people. It can cause leadership discouragement and failure. Perhaps Joshua remembered the link between Moses' failure and the Israelites' rebellion (Nu. 20:1-13). The pieces were coming together. There was an interrelationship between God's people, a network of holy relations, that must be maintained. As an individual his private actions, whether good or bad, affected the course of corporate life. As a leader, he was called to foster an environment of harmonious relationships that would engender Yahweh's blessings. This incident was a demonstration in the school of life of the relationship between sin and the release of God's power. One person in sin can block the flow of divine blessing. Disobedience of a single follower to explicit commands, concerning a specific situation, can stop God's power for the entire body of believers. This type of selfishness will disintegrate community.

Process Item 2: Word Check

In Joshua 9, Joshua failed one word check, but passed another. God had directed the Israelites to dispossess and exterminate the residents of Canaan, and to refrain from making treaties with them (Ex. 23:31-33 34:12; Deut. 7:2). This word had been clearly communicated to Joshua, and yet he made a pact with the Gibeonites. Friendship was vowed to the enemies of God. It was an act in disobedience to Moses' words in Deuteronomy 7:1,2: "You shall make no covenant with them and show no mercy to them." Joshua knew this word. However, the Gibeonites planned a detailed deception. Their "spiritual" testimony must have sounded much like Rahab's confession of faith rather than the false flattery it really was (vv. 9-13) (Davis 1988:77). Because of this convincing demonstration, Joshua was drawn into deception.

God's stern injunction was, "No covenant and no mercy." This was just the opposite of what Joshua did. Peace was made with the Gibeonites, transforming their physical proximity into peaceful coexistence (Hamlin 1983:82). Furthermore, a covenant was ratified (9:25). This meant more than peaceful coexistence for it included mutual defense, mutual assistance, and mutual responsibility (Hamlin 1983:82). Thus the foreigners were allowed to share the same options that Israel had for life in the land. On the dark side, it meant an infusion of tainted blood into the circulatory system of God's covenant body.

It's no accident that this word check followed (in the Canon of scripture) the covenant renewal at Mount Ebal (Josh. 8). At Mount Ebal God's word had just been rehearsed, the blessings and curses narrated. This high point of ceremony celebrating Yahweh must have been accompanied by high levels of renewed commitment, both by Joshua and the people. But the sincerity of this commitment was to be tested. Along came the Gibeonites who acted with "cunning" (v.4). A word with the same root describes the "cunning" of the serpent in Genesis 3:1. The suggestion is that hidden within the Gibeonites' "request for an alliance is the fatal attraction of Canaanite culture" (Hamlin 1983:80). In a sense, the seductions of this age were laying a deadly trap, catching its prey in the snare of spiritual compromise.

What happened? Had Joshua failed to meditate in The Book as God instructed (Josh. 1:8a)? Had he become careless in its practical applications? Possibly, for God's promised success eluded him (Josh. 1:8c). He experienced a major failure in his dealings with the Gibeonites.

But failure can lead to an opportunity to prove oneself true. Joshua could have allowed this mistake to cause a downward spiral. One lapse can easily lead to another. But this didn't happen. Joshua honored the pact with the Gibeonites based on Moses' command, "When a man...takes an oath to obligate himself to a pledge he must do everything he said" (Nu. 30:2). The recovered leader would not compromise this word. He understood its practical applications for his present situation. He courageously stood his ground.

One word check was immediately followed by another check. In properly dealing with the consequences of his initial failure Joshua gained new ground and upheld the standards of integrity and honor. A leadership failure was transformed into an honorable leadership act. Lack of discernment in the first check was countered by discernment in the second. Obscured truth (God said, "No covenant; no mercy") gave way to clarification of truth (We have given them our oath...we cannot touch them now). God was fine tuning Joshua's ability to understand and apply His word.

Process Item 3: Spiritual Authority Discovery

Three experiences stimulated Joshua's movement from one degree of spiritual authority to another. These experiences included a theophany (Josh. 5:13-6:5), a crisis (Josh. 7), and a supernatural victory (Josh. 8:1-29). The important elements in these incidents included the divine presence, a word from the Lord, and obedience to that word along with God's response.

In Joshua 5:13-6:5 Joshua discovered the essential source of all authority, God[36] A revelation of the Lord of Hosts taught him that the weight of ultimate responsibility was not upon his shoulders. His authority came from a higher source. Spiritual authority was the outcome of this meeting with God (vv.13,14a). Reverent submission and total commitment plugged Joshua into the power source (vv.14b,15). As a result of this meeting, Joshua knew who the real commander was. God gave him the battle strategy for Jericho's defeat, A miraculous victory was the outcome.

In Joshua 7, a crisis situation required spiritual sensitivity and bold obedience. Joshua's ability to hear God, discern the situation, and lead the people out from under divine wrath increased the depth of his influence among the Israelites. Here was one who was not only competent and legitimate, but also one who had superior spirituality, who demonstrated spiritual maturity and an ability to incarnate God's will for a specific situation. The Israelites were discovering the depth of leadership quality in this man. God was continuing to establish him in the eyes of the people.

Joshua, on the other hand, was learning that God was "calling the shots." His own expertise wouldn't get the job done. Ai couldn't be won by his fine abilities. Yahweh was in charge. Joshua was only a channel for divine authority. The success or failure of the nation depended upon his obedient submission to the Lord who was in charge.

In Joshua 8, victory was the outcome of leadership submitted to and empowered by God (Josh. 8). Where there had once been defeat because of sin

---

36.Spiritllal authority has its ultimate source in God. Bobby calls this the Ultimate Source (Clinton 1989:194). Joshua had early lessons about this aspect of spiritual authority in Exodus 24:9-1833.

(Josh. 7), there was now triumph because of righteousness (Josh. 8). There was expansion after purification. One man's false step (ch. 7) became an opportunity for growth (ch. 8). Joshua likely learned that it's God's responsibility to defend spiritual authority. God will back a leader who willingly places himself/herself under divine rule.

In the same incident, God told Joshua, "Hold out toward Ai the javelin that is in your hand" (Josh. 8:18). As soon as Joshua obeyed, the victory was won. A symbolic action, similar to Moses' upraised hands in Exodus 17:11-13, was a sign of the supernatural nature of this conquest. Although natural means were used, victory was not in the javelin but in the Lord. Again, the parallel to Moses reminded the people that the same God who was with Moses was also with Joshua.

Process Item 4: Word Item

God spoke a word to Joshua which affected his decisions in a difficult situation (Josh. 7:10-15). In the perplexity and despair of defeat at Ai , Joshua tore his clothes, fell down on the ground, and began to pray (vv.6-9). God responded, disclosing the nature of the problem and the appropriate course of action. This word gave Joshua understanding of the situation: "Israel has sinned" (v.ll). It provided knowledge of the problem: "Israel has sinned...that is why the Israelites cannot stand" (v.12). And it conveyed God's wisdom on how to deal with the problem, a step-by-step procedure for rectifying the situation (vv. 13-15). Thus Joshua skillfully guided the Israelites through the maze of confusion and uncertainty.

Joshua proved himself capable of discerning Yahweh's voice in the vice grip of despair and defeat. God's word was an accurate guide and helpful decision-malting tool. The demonstration of Joshua's ability to discern God's voice and apply divine wisdom for a national problem increased his credibility among the Israelites. Consequently, Joshua was able to transform failure into a springboard to deeper levels of influence.

In another incident, Joshua had an opportunity to apply God's written and spoken word (Josh. 10). A treaty had been made with the Gibeonites in the previous chapter. God's written word required Joshua to honor this treaty (cf. Nu. 30:2). In light of this word, he must have felt compelled to respond to the Gibeonites' appeal for assistance. As he responded, God spoke and assured him of victory (v.8). The divine promise confirmed Joshua's involvement in this affair, and revealed God's intention. As he proceeded to help the Gibeonites he experienced a unique demonstration of divine power (v.14), tremendous affirmation (v.21), and a series of successful conquests (vv.25,29-43).

Another word affected Joshua's military decisions (Josh. 11). A crisis occurred when a coalition of northern kings initiated military action against Israel (vv. 1-5). It was a critical time. Again, Joshua proved leadership maturity in his ability to discern God's voice. God gave him needed encouragement, a promise of victory, and brief instructions (v.6). This word served as an energizing support. It was a road sign along the battle route to conquest.

Process Item 5: Literary Item

The Book of the Law played a central role in Joshua's life. Immediately after the victory at Ai (Josh. 8:1-29), Joshua and the Israelites were found at Mount Ebal, more than twenty miles away (Josh. 8:30-35). Joshua had the Book of the Law and was carefully following its instructions. This sudden shift from conquest to covenant underscores the fact that "heeding God's word is more crucial than fighting God's war. By placing this covenant renewal ceremony here, the writer is saying that Israel's success does not primarily consist in knocking off Canaanites but in everyone's total submission to the word of God" (Davis 1988:72).

Here was a book that was a key element in Joshua's life. It was more than a mentor's memoirs; it was God's revelation to His people. It was so important that it became the national focus. Joshua wrote the law on plastered stones for public display, reminiscent of the tablets of stone Moses carried down from Mount Sinai. This book was the foundation to all of Joshua's conquest efforts.

Process Item 6: Destiny Revelation

The Lord appeared to Joshua identifying Himself as commander of the army of the Lord (Josh. 5:13-6:5).[37] This theophany was consistent with past revelations. In the Exodus, God revealed Himself as the God of war (Ex. 14:24,25). At Rephidim Moses named an altar, "The Lord is my Banner." Joshua was familiar with the war-God. Now he was meeting this One face-to-face. These disclosures of the divine character were consistently tailored to fit Joshua's upcoming military role and assignment. In revealing Himself in this way, Yahweh was revealing the nature of Joshua's calling.

A profound sense of God's presence was revolutionizing Joshua's life. God was strengthening him for war that loomed only hours away. Before Joshua stood the true leader of Israel's army with a raised sword. That raised sword meant God was going to fight on his behalf. His destiny entailed conquest

---

37.It is generally accepted that this incident was a theophany. Hughes gives three reasons for believing this.

> First, Joshua was told to take off his shoes, and this very same command was given to Moses by God from the burning bush.... Joshua is to realize, through this command, that the One who speaks is the same God who spoke to Moses. Second, the 'captain of the host' who speaks to Joshua is identified as the Lord in the instructions He gives in 6:2-5, introduced by 'And the Lord said to Joshua....' Third, as Origen said in his Sixth Homily on Joshua, 'Joshua knew not only that he was of God, but that he was God. For he would not have worshipped him, had he not recognized him to be God" (Hughes 1987:65).

wrought by the sword of the Lord. This unique awareness of God marked him as a leader with a special destiny.

Process Item 7: Faith Challenge

Joshua faced at least two faith challenges during this period: the capture of Jericho (Josh. 6), and the battle at Ai (Josh. 8). In each of these instances God gave a specific word composed of direction and promise. Each time Joshua was challenged to act on the basis of God's word. Both times he moved in faith. His faith steps were met with divine affirmation and ministry achievement in such a way that Joshua's faith capacity was enlarged (Clinton 1989:222).

At Jericho, Joshua faced the impossible (Josh. 6). Jericho was "tightly shut up" symbolizing, not only impregnability, but also collective pride against God (v.l) (Hamlin 1983:49). But the note of impossibility in verse one was followed by God's word of promise: "I have delivered Jericho into your hands" (v.2). Promise was then followed by divine direction (vv.3-5).

Joshua was being challenged to do the impossible, much like he had been challenged at the Jordan River. But this time he had an experiential basis for faith. Through his experience at the river, faith had been ripened for the seemingly incredulous conquest instructions (vv.3-5). Joshua obeyed these instructions and reaped the result of faith's triumph, a ministry achievement. Jericho was conquered, not merely by military expertise but by Yahweh's assistance.

At Jericho, Joshua learned some important faith lessons. He learned that a challenge from God must be met with implicit obedience (vv.12-16). Faith's focus must be on the reality of God's abiding presence as represented by the central position of the ark (v.6) (Hughes 1987:74). He also learned that faith is best exercised from a position of total dependence. The futility of marching around Jericho thirteen times must have impressed him with the impossibility of the situation (v.14) (Hughes 1987:78,79). Finally, Joshua was learning that faith will proclaim itself in confident declaration (v.20) (Hughes 1987:79,80), Possibly he had learned this from Rahab's confession of faith (Josh.2:9,11). An accumulation of Joshua's past experiences merged in this incident. The result was a triumphant response to a significant challenge. Jericho's wall fell in its place (v.20).[38]

The second faith challenge at Ai (Josh. 8) was especially difficult due to the fresh wounds of defeat that had been inflicted there (cf. Josh. 7). Joshua had just experienced his first military failure in Canaanite conquest. It was a humbling experience and one that probably dealt a blow to any element of self-confidence. In a chastened frame of mind, Joshua received God's word

---

38. Hughes suggests four faith factors in this incident at Jericho. They are the obedience of faith. the focus of faith, the dependence of faith, and the declaration of faith (Hughes 1987:74-80).

with a readiness to obey (Josh. 8:1). God's word was a challenge to conquer those who had administered defeat. But in the midst of what might be a difficult command, God gave the promise of victory and a foundation for faith. God Mid, "I have delivered into your hands the king of Ai, his people, his city and his land" (v. 1c).

One result of this challenge was to catapult Joshua and the Israelites out of the depression and discouragement produced by failure (cf. Josh. 7:5-9). Defeat can have a debilitating effect and God didn't want this to happen. Joshua had taken the appropriate steps in dealing with Achan's sin, and now God seemed to say, "Alright, let's get on with the program. We did it before. We can do it again. I'm the one who gives the victory. Victory will come when you operate according to my terms.

While the defeat of Jericho looked impossible, the Israelites were victorious. On the other hand, the defeat of Ai looked probable, but an initial attempt at conquest failed. Joshua was learning an oft repeated lesson about the nature of his warfare: God is the one who gives the victory. The failure at Ai forced dependence upon Yahweh and a realignment of faith's focus.

Process Item 8: Prayer Challenge

The conquest period was primarily a "doing" phase.[39] The emphasis was on Joshua's activity as a leader. He was busy with war. But in the midst of a hectic leadership pace God captured his attention. Busyness with military activities and schemes probably warranted a fresh call to prayer. How does God gain an active leader's attention? God got Joshua's attention through a military flop (Josh. 7). Defeat brought him quickly to the Lord (vv.6,7). God revealed Achan's sin as the cause of military failure. Surely Joshua must have been impressed with the necessity to pray for those in his charge. After all, if the one man, Achan, could cause this much trouble, he had better take his prayer responsibility seriously. Military protection was not enough to safely lead these people. They needed the guardian of intercession. Yes, the Lord was their captain and guide, but even this fact didn't negate the leadership call to prayer.

Process Item 9: Power Item

In at least two situations power items were evident. The first incident occurred in Joshua 5:13-6:5. The commander of the Lord's army appeared to Joshua prior to the battle at Jericho. Joshua must have understood the significance of the moment: it was clear that power for leadership comes from the Lord. God's support of Joshua's ministry was evident. This reality must have been impressed upon the Israelites when they learned of the heavenly encoun-

39."During certain times processing focuses on leadership character ('beingness'). At other times processing emphasizes leadership skills ('doingness')" (Clinton 1989:376).

ter. The encounter was wonderfully similar to Moses' experience at the burning bush; both events marked an entrance into God's calling. What a convincing act of power, persuading and reassuring followers of the divine origin of Joshua's leadership.

The second power item was a negative experience, a hard lesson about hindrances to God's power. The Israelites suffered their first defeat at Ai because of one man's sin (Josh. 7). Power for victory returned only after purity was restored. Joshua learned that God's power can be blocked by sin. One person out of harmony with God can stop the flow of divine might. In order for power to be restored, a holy harmony among God's people must be maintained.

Process Item 10: Prayer Power

The five kings of the Amorites formed a coalition against the Gibeonites because of their alliance with Israel (Josh. 10). The Gibeonites sent word to Joshua asking for help v.6). He immediately responded (v.7). The Lord assured him of victory (v.8). A battle ensued (vv. 9-10) and the enemies were routed (v.11). In the midst of this triumphant turmoil Joshua experienced a dynamic demonstration of divine power in response to prayer (vv.12-14).

The relationship here between prayer and conquest is roughly reminiscent of Yahweh's intervention at Rephidim (Ex. 17:8-16). The same power that had been released through Joshua's mentor, Moses, now flowed in his own life. God answered prayer, demonstrating the authenticity of Joshua's spiritual authority.

The prayer was more of a command than a petition. Joshua ordered, "O sun, stand still over Gibeon, O moon, over the valley of Aijalon" (v.12b). He spoke to the elements much like Jesus had spoken to the turbulent seas (cf. Mk. 4:35-41). The sun and the moon stopped at his command. Prayer power required commanding power. Not only was Joshua a commander in Israel's army, he was also a commander in the spiritual realm. His sphere of influence not only extended into the natural realm but into the spiritual as well.

Process Item 11: Crisis

Joshua probably experienced many crises during the conquest period; however, three stand out as particularly significant. At Ai an internal crisis, sin, produced an external crisis, defeat (Josh. 7). The external turmoil was an indicator of an internal problem. God used this crisis to purify Israel and to demonstrate the importance of holiness. It also served to test Joshua's dependence upon God. This was an appropriate follow-up to the overwhelming victory at Jericho. Had there been any pride or sense of self-accomplishment surrounding Joshua's fame, it would have been quickly dashed to pieces on the rock of failure (Josh. 7).

Another crisis surfaced when the five Amorite kings positioned themselves against the Gibeonites (Josh. 10: 1-15). Because of a treaty made with the Gibeonites this crisis became Israel's crisis. God used this situation to teach Joshua dependence and to impress him with divine sovereignty. Here was a group of people who had mastered a major deception campaign against Israel, and yet God gave a mighty demonstration of delivering power on their behalf. Joshua learned that God can meet him in the entangled affairs of life with a tailor-made solution.

In Joshua 11 the northern kings formed a massive power structure in an effort to defeat the Israelites. This initial threat marked the beginning of a long struggle lasting many years. The result was a series of crises in which the opposing powers waged war against Israel (v.20). The hardening of the kings' hearts (v. 20) described the resistance of "oppressive institutional structures to liberating changes" (Hamlin 1983:103). This resistance created a continual tension that would have pressed Joshua into a habitual dependence mould. These conditions would require a lifestyle wholly abandoned to the power and presence of Yahweh. Such abandonment would prove worthwhile, for God gave the victory a little at a time until Joshua took the land (v. 23). These crises were responsible for developing the posture necessary to move Joshua into unique ministry.

Process Item 12: Divine Affirmation

One intention of the Lord's personal encounter with Joshua was to give divine approval and reassurance (Josh. 5:13-6:5). Joshua had taken the preliminary steps to conquest (Josh 1-592). Now the formidable city, Jericho, stood before him. Warfare was about to begin. Joshua needed the inner power of a personal revelation, the support of an encounter with the living God. He'd often seen God fight for Israel, but it was time to meet the heavenly warrior face-to-face.

Joshua's earthly model, Moses, was gone, but now he had the heavenly model, the commander of the Lord's army. As he had faithfully followed Moses, now he was to follow the Lord.[40] This was a turning point in his life. It's likely that this was the pivot point at which Joshua became identified as the servant of the Lord rather than the servant of Moses. If this was the case, the divine encounter became the hinge of life that opened the door to the biblical testimony, "Joshua son of Nun, the servant of the Lord" (Josh. 24:29).

This incident also revealed a four-fold pattern of affirmation for a major faith challenge. This pattern included a revelation of the Lord, a realization

---

40.Hollander claims that being "a leader and being a follower are not inconsistent with each other " (1978:5). Those most desired as leaders and those most desired as followers are often the same people. While emphasis is usually given to "leadership qualities," it might be "followership qualities" which are recognized first (1978:6).

that it is the Lord who will fight for us, submissive worship of the Lord, and guidance from God. Each of these elements were important as Joshua faced the challenges of conquest. With the strength of divine affirmation he proceeded to Jericho where God gave an overwhelming victory.

Process Item 13: Ministry Affirmation

Ministry affirmations came in the form of military successes. The defeat of Jericho was followed by the biblical affirmation, "So the Lord was with Joshua, and his fame spread throughout the land" (Josh 6:27). There was a sense of divine approval associated with this campaign. Joshua had listened to, and obeyed, God. A supernatural victory was the result. Its impact reverberated throughout the land. His sphere of influence expanded beyond the Israelite nation into Canaanite territory. The international recognition of his quality leadership must have encouraged Joshua.

In his march against the five Amorite kings God intervened in a supernatural way (Josh. 10:1-28). The highlight of this intervention centered around Joshua's prayer and its stunning results (vv. 12-13). Not only were the opposing forces unable to withstand him (v. 18), but they had never seen such a remarkable demonstration of power and authority in prayer. Two affirmations were bestowed upon him in this military endevour. First, the Bible says, "There has never been a daylike it before or since, a day when the Lord listened to a man" (v.14). God was placing the divine seal of approval upon Joshua's spritual leadership. Second, an almost incidental statement was inserted in the biblical record, "No one uttered a word against the Israelites" (v.21b). So powerful was the impact of Joshua's leadership and Israel's army, that people stood in awe. Military success must have given Joshua a renewed sense of purpose, a sense of purpose much needed after his leadership failure with the Gibeonites (Josh.9).

Joshua 10:29-43 and Joshua 11 record a rapid succession of military successes, first in the southern cities of Canaan and then against the northern kings. In the southern battles,"all these kings and their lands Joshua conquered in one campaign, because the Lord, the Gosd of Israel, fought for Israel" (10:42). God had assured Joshua of His presence time and again, but military accomplishment was the visible crown affirming that presence. Conquest was a sign that God was with Joshua. In the battle account against the northern kings a key affirmation was given,"Joshua took the entire land" (11;16,23). Joshua did what he had been called and commissioned to do.

Finally, chapter twelve lists Joshua's military accomplishments. Joshua and the Israelites conquered thirty-one kings in all (Josh. 12:24b). There must have been deep inner satisfaction as Joshua reflected on this military history. HIs job was by no means done, but in retrospect he was able to see how God had planned and unfolded a remarkable history. What an encouragement this would be as he later faced the task of organizing life on the Land (Josh. 13-19).

Process Item 14: Flesh Act

Joshua's treaty with the Gibeonites was a flesh act that had corporate ramifications (Josh. 9). He assumed the Gibeonites were from a distant land, but
they actually lived nearby. They deliberately established a false identity to
avoid a destruction similar to that at Jericho and Ai (v.3), as well as in the
trans Jordan kingdoms (v.10). Joshua believed their deception and vowed
friendship with God's enemies. This covenant was in direct disobedience to
Moses' injunction in Deuteronomy 7:1,2. Joshua experienced a major leadership failure.

The reason for this failure is clear. Joshua and his leaders did not inquire
of the Lord (v.14). "It was not that they were sloppy in their investigation but
that they were alone in their decision. It wasn't that they didn't think but that
they didn't pray" (Davis 1988:77). They did not seek God's counsel when
deciding to establish an important treaty with another people.

In that moment when Joshua "did not ask counsel of the Lord,"
he was forgetting his very first leadership lesson under Moses,
when he saw the tide of battle against the Amalekites ebb and
flow with the fall and rise of Moses' intercessory hands (Exodus
17:8-16). He forgot that prayer holds the greatest importance for
spiritual leadership (Hughes 1987:108).

As a result, an alien element was introduced into the Israelite community.
A group of idolatrous people were incorporated into God's holy system. Ever
present would be the possiblity of an evil, leavening influence in their midst.
The quality of community life was jeopardized by one false act.

In retrospect Joshua was probably learning some very important lessons.
All things are not what they may appear to be. God's requirements, that had
just been rehearsed on Mount Ebal (Josh. 8), were to be obeyed. However,
obedience requires discernment and spiritual insight. It's one thing to have the
written code, but quite another to discern its application on a situational basis.
A leader needs spiritual insight. Major decisions cannot be presumed. They
must be taken before the Lord in prayer. One must depend upon God at all
times because deceptive forces are at work to thwart the purposes of God.

Although Joshua made a mistake, he did not allow his error to affect the
continuing quality of his leadership (vv.16-21). He exhibited a mature leadership skill: the ability to turn a failure into a success. That which could have
destroyed credibility was used to build the same.[41] Joshua demonstrated leadership strength by facing his failure, dealing with it immediately, not taking the
easy way out, and maintaining integrity in spite of the cost. These qualities
distinguish a noble leader from a mediocre one.

Immediately following this incident was one of the most dramatic miracles ever recorded in scripture (Josh. 10: 12-14). Joshua prayed, commanding the sun and moon to stand still (v.12). The elements responded (v.13). It was a miracle. It seemed that God was using Joshua's leadership failure in chapter nine as a humbling experience prior to this dramatic demonstration of spiritual power. The principle is that God gives grace to the humble (cf. I Peter. 5:5).

Process Item 15: Destiny Fulfillment

Joshua was beginning to see the completion of specific aspects of his destiny. Destiny fulfillment came through promise realization, obedience processing, and prophecy fulfillment. These fulfillment items merged to give closure to the conquest portion of Joshua's assignment.

Many *divine promises* were being realized. In Joshua 1, God gave at least four promises: He would give Joshua every place he set his foot (v. 3) no one would be able to withstand him (v. 5a); God would be with Joshua as He had been with Moses (v. 5b); and a general sense of God's presence was assured (v. 9b). These all found fulfillment throughout the conquest. Every place Joshua went in Canaan became the divine gift (11:23). No one was able to withstand his military campaigns (cf. Josh. 6;8:1-29;10;11). God's presence was manifest in ways surprisingly similar to Moses (cf. Josh. 5:13-6:5; 8:18,19). And there were many statements affirming Yahweh's presence (Josh. 6:27;10:10, 14,42).

Obedience processing was an important aspect of destiny fulfillment. Joshua had been commissioned to carry out the vision communicated by Moses. Joshua obeyed Moses' directives. "As the Lord commanded his servant Moses, so Moses commanded Joshua, and Joshua did it; he left nothing undone of all that the Lord commanded Moses" (1195). In obeying Moses' instructions Joshua was fulfilling his destiny.

One significant instruction given to Joshua was to destroy the conquered nations. The seven nations were to be destroyed (Deut. 7:2) because they would "turn your sons away from following me" (Deut. 7:4), and "they will teach you to follow all the detestable things they do in worshipping their gods, and you will sin against the Lord your God" (Deut. 20:18). Joshua executed this destruction at Jericho (Josh. 6:24), Ai (Josh. 8:26), Makkedah, Eglon, Hebron, Debir (10:28,35,37,39), Hazer and the areas of the northern confeder-

---

41.Although the Israelites grumbled about Joshua's decision to honor the treaty with the Gibeonites, I believe this act actually enhanced Joshua's authority and influence among the people. A follower's ties to a leader depend on how the leader's actions and motives are perceived (Holiander 1978:39). Joshua addressed Israel's perception of his action in Josh. 9:19. He said, "We have given them [the Gibeonites] our oath by the Lord, the God of Israel, and we cannot touch them now." The Israelites initially perceived his decision as weakness. but he showed them that it was an indication of integrity and strength.

acy (11:11-12), the Anakim and their cities (11:21), and throughout the entire land (10:40: 11:20) (Hamlin 1983:53). Destiny fulfillment came through radical obedience.

At his commissioning, Joshua received *prophetic insight* (cf. Deut. 31; Josh. 1:1-9). Moses prophetically described Joshua's involvement in possessing the Land, and compared the future conquest to the defeat of Sihon and Og (Deut. 31:3-8). Joshua's role in Israel's national destiny was also foreseen (Deut. 31:23). God clarified the parameters of Israel's future inheritance, and indicated the territorial extent of Joshua's militsrv influence (Josh. 1:4). Military campaigns succeeded as foretold (Josh. 6), and much of the designated territory had been taken by Joshua (Josh. 11:16-23;12:7-24).

Sub-phase C: Establishing the Land

In this portion of Joshua's life his assigned task came to completion. Previous experiences prepared him for the multi-faceted leadership required during this time. A new sub-phase was signaled by a significant passage of time (Josh. 13:1) and a shift in emphasis. While battles continued to be fought, it was no longer primarily a time of war. There was rest in the Land (Josh. 11:23b). Settlement became the issue. It was an issue that required diversified leadership. War demanded a singular focus, but settlement required attention in many directions. Joshua had to "wear many hats" to be a suitable leader at this time. It was an opportunity for flexibility. He was able to draw upon many past skills and former roles. These were drawn together to create a unique ministry. The end of this sub-phase was marked by a passage of time (Josh. 23:1) and Joshua's realization that the closing moments of his life were fast approaching,

The major process items in this sub-phase include the following:

1. Ideal Role Discovery
2. Influence Mix Discovery
3. Destiny Fulfillment

Process Item I: Ideal Role Discovery

The task of establishing the Land called for a harmonious blending of past roles into a unique, seasoned leadership function. Foundational to this function was the servant role.[42] Earlier in his career Joshua had spent many years as Moses' servant or aide. In a sense he continued to be subject to Moses' direction throughout his lifetime, doing the bidding of his deceased mentor. However, as Joshua matured there was a shift in this servant function. As a final testimony he was identified as "Joshua son of Nun, the servant of the Lord" (Josh. 24:29).[43]   The one who had been the servant of Moses, became the servant of the Lord. The laborious, not so exciting task, of land distribu-

---

42. See Bobby's notes on "4 Biblical Leadership Models" (Clinton 1989:56-61).

43. Many years earlier, in Exodus 24:13, Joshua was identified as Moses' "aide" or servant.

tion, management and government would require a deep commitment to ser-vanthood.

A leadership shift seems to have occurred between the conquest and estab-lishment periods. Throughout the conquest Joshua exhibited a strong, central leadership. This was not the case when it came time to settle the Land. A decentralization of power apparently took place.[44] "Eleazar the priest, Joshua the son of Nun, and the heads of the tribal clans of Israel" were responsible for the land allotment (Josh. 14:1b; 21:1,2). Joshua was a leader (still probably the primary leader) among a company of leaders. However, team leadership was not new to him. Years earlier, on Mount Sinai (Ex. 24:9-18), he had been part of a leadership conglomerate. He knew what it meant to function in a coopera-tive role with other leaders. This was now important in establishing the land. In the Israelite pattern of land management God was the ultimate owner.[45] The land was to be distributed to all the people and not to one ruler, as had been the Canaanite practice (Hamlin 1983:110). Thus, the diffusion of power during this time served to enhance God's design for a new society.

Joshua also drew from his past experiences as an administrator. As an aide to Moses he had been called upon to organize and implement his visionary mentors instructions. In fact, Joshua's life assignment was to carry out the divine purposes as they had been perceived and communicated by Moses. The focus of Joshua's leadership was the implementation of these instructions. While Joshua received directions from Yahweh during this period, no new cor-porate direction or purpose was revealed. Joshua basically functioned on the past revelations communicated through Moses.

Joshua's former role as military commander was also significant in estab-lishing the land. While he was probably no longer involved in actual conquest, he was able to exert indirect military influence. He encouraged and directed tribal conquest activities. For example, to the tribes of Ephraim and Manasseh he said, "Though the Canaanites have iron chariots and though they are strong you can drive them out" (Josh. 17:18).

Finally, all of these previous functions merged into a new role, that of arbi-trator and statesman. Joshua was engaged in arbitrating land settlement and in

---

44. It's possible that decentralization began in seed form as a result of Moses' actions. Moses assigned Eleazar to a prominent position alongside Joshua (Nu. 27:21). Also, when Moses gave irtstructions about conquering and establishing the Land, he addressed himself to a group of leaders and not just Joshua (Nu. 32:28). Thus, this form of leadership could have been encour-aged by Moses himself.

45. Hamlin identifies two patterns of land management: the Canaan and israel patterns. The Canaan pattern contrasts the Israel pattern in that only a small percentage of the people, in the Canaan pattern, control a large part of the production means. and most of the people are exploited for the benefit of a few (1983:109-110). The implication is that Joshua was in charge of establishing the new pattern of land management.

leading national and international affairs. Along with other leaders, he allotted tribal territories according to their kinship associations. This ensured financial protection for the poorer members, and military protection for all.[46] He dealt with environmental issues (Josh. 17:14-18) and served as an arbitrator of territorial claims (Josh. 9).[47] At God's behest he established cities of refuge as part of the legal system to protect against the vices of injustice (Josh. 20). An educational program was also set up. In Joshua 21 levitical cities were established. These "might be called Torah Centers, i.e, places where God's Teaching would be studied, interpreted, practiced, and taught (cf. Josh. 8:30-35)" (Hamlin 1983:140). All of these functions were a necessary part of Joshua's task. They were necessary to the success of the entire process of inheriting, possessing, and finding rest in the land.

Process Item 2: Influence Mix Discovery

Establishing the Land marks a period of mature influence in Joshua's life. It was at this juncture that he experienced an ideal influence mix.[48]

He exerted intimate, direct influence among the circle of leaders that emerged (Josh. 14:1b). He was probably the primary leader among the group. As such, he was able to impact their leadership. Indirect national influence was also a result. These leaders whom he was affecting would in turn influence national life.

Direct and indirect national influence continued to be exercised. Direct influence occurred as Joshua interacted with the tribes of Israel (Josh. 17:14-18;18:3-10). Both direct and indirect types were used in the establishment of a social structure within the land. Joshua helped his people become an organized, cohesive society. This directly impacted the Israelites of his day, and indirectly influenced the quality of life for years to come. He created a structure upon which future generations could build.

Large organizational influence was evident in the various roles assigned to Joshua. The organizational structure of the nation took shape as the result of his leadership influence.

Finally, indirect international influence was felt. In establishing the land, the tribes were given specific geographic locations. These areas housed inhabitants from many other nations. The inhabitants were being influenced by the

---

46. See note five.

47. According to Hamlin, the people of Joseph were to turn their forested inheritance into a park (Josh. 17:15,17). He states that Joshua's command to "clear" the ground means to "cocreate or participat in God's creative act by transforming the forest thicket into a forest park, i.e, making it habitable, life supporting, and beautiful" (1983:129).

48. "The exercise of influence by organizational leaders has the two main goals of task success and group maintenance" (Hollander 1978:89). The purpose of Joshua's matured influence at this time seemed to be for the maintenance of God's goals for Israel..

infiltration of a conquering nation. Many lives would never be the same. The character of the land was being transformed by the inroads of invasion. All of this was occurring as an indirect result of Joshua's leadership. Extensive, although not intensive, influence was being exerted on the surrounding cultures.

Process Item 3: Destiny Fulfillment

Destiny fulfillment was significant during this time. Joshua was seeing a wrap-up of many destiny items, both for himself and for his people. Rest in the land was the goal of his life assignment, and that rest was in the making.

The scriptures indicate that "not one of the Lord's good promises to the house of Israel failed; every one was fulfilled" (Josh. 21:45). Joshua saw the fulfillment of a personal and corporate destiny. The Lord gave the land which he swore to his fathers (cf. Josh. 21:4; 1:6). Joshua took possession of it (cf. Josh.21:43;1:11). The Lord gave rest (cf. Josh. 21:44;1:5). His enemies were given into his hands (cf. Josh. 21:44; 2:24). All of the Lord's promises came to pass (Josh. 21:45). And God had been with Joshua as He had promised (Josh. 1:9b).

Joshua fulfilled his destiny, and brought Israel into her inheritance (Josh. 21:45). But although he completed his task, much remained to be done. Why this apparent contradiction? Because God intended that the acquisition of this inheritance be a gradual process. Exodus 23:29 gives one reason why: "I will not drive them out before you in one year, otherwise, the land would become desolate and the wild beasts multiply against you." Another reason was proposed in Judges 3:1,2: "These are the nations the Lord left to test all those Israelites who had not experienced any of the wars of Canaan (he did this only to teach warfare to the descendants of the Israelites who had not had previous battle experience). The unconquered territories represented God's design and not necessarily Joshua's failure. Joshua had done what the Lord required of him (Josh. 11:15).

Subphase D: Retaining the Land

Retaining the Land was a period of afterglow that may have lasted up to ten years (Hughes 1987:147). The beginning of this segment in Joshua's life was indicated by a passage of time (Josh. 23:1), the reflective nature of Joshua's speeches, and the fact that he was anticipating his death (Josh. 23:2,4). He had fulfilled the divine commission for his life and was coming to the closing moments of his destiny.

Out of the reservoir of life, Joshua drew his two final speeches (Josh 23,24). In these speeches he directed the people back to God's promises. They were the same promises God had given him. The promise and presence that had provided him with continuity would provide the Israelites with continuity. His exhortation to obey the Law of Moses (v.6) was the same word God had given him years earlier (Josh. 1:8). The call to "cleave to" and "love" the Lord was an appeal to maintain their first love (vv.8,11). How important this love had been to Joshua! He was probably recalling sweet memories of communion with God in the tabernacle (Ex. 33:7-11). And finally, as Moses had left Joshua with a written legacy; so Joshua left a written record of the Israelites' commitment to Yahweh (Josh. 24:25). In the future they were to remember this commitment. These moments embraced reflections of the past as well as anticipations of the future.

The only process item identifiable during this period is destiny fulfillment.

Process Item I: Destiny Fulfillment

As a final destiny act, Joshua assembled the Israelites together at Shechem (Josh. 24). It was at Shechem that God had promised Abram, "To your offspring I will give this land" (Gen. 12:7) (Davis 1988:204). Now, five or six hundred years later Joshua, in a public act, stood in that very place of promise, symbolizing fulfillment of a long awaited destiny for a nation. Joshua had completed his destiny and led a nation into a significant level of destiny attainment. It's no accident that this marked Joshua's departure from the biblical scene. The location of this final assembly was a declaration of God's faithfulness and Joshua's leadership as a man of destiny.

Afterglow Afterthoughts

Afterglow is a time of celebration, celebration of a lifetime of service for the Lord. It is generally a time in which the fruit of one's life and ministry culminates in a season of recognition and indirect influence at broad levels (Clinton 1988:47).

Joshua had built up a lifetime of contacts and credibility. He continued to exert influence in his relationships with the Israelites and her leaders. A storehouse of wisdom had been gathered, and with this wisdom he blessed and counseled the people (Josh. 23,24).

At this time of celebration, during the final years of his life, Joshua exerted influence intended to impact upcoming generations. His speech in chapter twenty-three was primarily directed toward the civil leaders of Israel (Hamlin 1983:179). Joshua knew that ongoing wholeness for the nation rested upon the shoulders of tomorrow's leadership. His influence upon them would indirectly affect the Israelites in years to come. The second assembly was addressed to all of Israel with the intention of influencing future behavior (Josh.24). This indirect influence was intended to shape the quality of life after his death. He also made a covenant, established decrees and laws (v.25), and recorded events in the Book of the Law (v.26a) with this end in mind. Finally, he set up a stone of witness, a telling reminder for years to come (v.26b). Because he was at the end of his life, the lateness of the hour urged him to utilize influence means that were not time bound.

As Joshua stood at the end of his journey of faith, glancing over the landscape of time, he probably had a sense of ultimate realities. All he had done was inconsequential apart from the love of Yahweh. In his role as servant, God had played an important part (Ex. 33:7-11). He wouldn't have had a role as military leader without God. Continued obedience to divine instructions had opened the door to military victory and to his roles as administrator and statesman. The vast experiences of a lifetime converged as Joshua assumed the role of spiritual leader.

As a spiritual leader he pointed the Israelites to God. Joshua instructed the elders and judges to cleave to and love the Lord (Josh. 23:8,11). It was an appeal to a deep personal attachment, an attachment that "springs from an awareness of the yearning love in the heart of the divine" (Hamlin 1983:187). Joshua was attempting to catalyze spiritual renewal. Then in chapter twenty-four, he stood before the people much like a seer, declaring a prophetic word (Josh. 24:2-13). Skillfully he wielded the double-edged sword of the Spirit, a commander in God's spiritual army. Like an evangelist he hooked the hearts of the people, reeling them in and landing them on the shores of sincere commitment (Josh. 24:14-24). And finally, like a priest he made a covenant for the people, and drew up decrees and laws (Josh. 24:25,26).

In his final days Joshua assumed a role in which he could wed spiritual certainties with life's realities. At this hour, the Israelites didn't need a commander, an administrator, or statesman. They needed a spiritual leader who could bring renewal, secure them in their faith, and point them toward a future with a destiny of blessing. God provided Joshua, the spiritual advisor.

Chart 7 Table of Principles Phase III

Name	Observation	Principle(s)
Crisis	1. During crises, Joshua recieved key words from the Lord (Joshua 7, 10, 11). 2. Two of the crises that Joshua faced during conquest as a result of sin (Joshua 7, 10).	1a. When facing crisis, a leader can expect God's assistance. 2a. The sin of both a follower and a leader can create a crisis among the community. 2b. Crises may be the result of sin.
Destiny Fulfillment	1. God's word to Joshua (Josh. 1:1-9) spurred him to action (Josh. 1-3), and initiaed destiny fulfillment. 2. In obedience to Moses' command, and in fulfilling his destiny, Joshua destroyed the cities he conquered (Deut. 7:2-4; Josh. 6:24; 8:8:26; 10:28).	1a. Sometimes giant steps of faith are required to move a leader into destiny fulfillment, creating a need for a strong catalyst and high levels of momentum. 1b. God's word can be this catalyst. 2a. Destiny fulfillment requires radical obedience.
Divine Affirmation	1. As Joshua came into leadership, God encouraged him with a prophetic word, a willing followership, a good report, and a demonstration of power (Josh. 1-3). 2. The Lord appeared to Joshua, revealing Himself as commander of the Lord's army (Josh. 5:13-6:5).	1a. Affirmations from God are particularly important during transition and when one's progress involves new and challenging events. 1b. Frequent affirmations accompany a leader entering into destiny fulfillment. 2a. A profound sense of God's presence revolutionizes a leader's attitude toward all of leadership. 2b. Leaders need a personal, inward affirmation from God. 2c. A personal revelation of God will produce inner power for leadership tasks. 2d. A significant encounter with God can be a leadership pivot point.
Failure	1. Joshua made a treaty with the Gibeonites contrary to God's will (Josh. 9). The result was the inclusion of a foreign nation into Israel's life. 2. This failure occurred after the ceremonial reading of the Law (Josh. 8, 9). 3. This failure was followed by a refusal to compromise his integrity. Joshua faced his failure and honored his treaty with the Gibeonites (Josh. 9:16-21). 4. After the Gibeonite failure, Joshua experienced one of the most dramatic miracles recorded in scripture (10:12-14).	1a. A leaders needs to be sure to have all the facts before making a decision. 1b. A leader should consult God in the decision making process. 1c. Leadership disobedience, whether intentional or unintentional, can have far reaching effects in the future well-being of followers. 2a. A leader can expect commitments to God's Word to be tested. 2b. Failure to meditate on God's word can result in a failure in leadership tasks. 3a. A good leader will guard against the spiraling effect of failure. 3b. A failure which destroys credibility can be used to build the same. 3c. A skillful leader will turn failure into a springboard for success. 3d. Healthy, spiritual leadership resists being stampeded by its failure. 3e. "Strong leadership returns to principle after its failure and does not compound the wrong by impulsive action" (Hughes, 1987:110). A leader must face failure, deal with it immediately, and maintain integrity throughout the process. 4a. God gives grace to the humble (I Peter 5:5).

Chart 7 Table of Principles Phase III cont.

NAME	OBSERVATION	PRINCIPLE(S)
Faith Challenges	1. In response to God's Word (Josh. 1:1-9), Joshua prepared the Israelites, sent spies into Jericho, and crossed the Jordan River (Josh. 1:10-18; 2; 3). 2. God led Israel across the Jordan at a time of year when crossing would be nearly impossible.	1a. Great steps of faith are required to step into a great destiny. 2a. In "...any challenging venture, the first step is always the hardest" (Hughes, 1987:25). 2b. A leader should expect God's affirmation of his/her faith responses. 2c. True faith will take aggressive steps outside of one's comfort zone. 2d. Full possession of God's promises requires ongoing steps of faith. 2e. God shows His might in the face of utter helplessness that He might be glorified (cf. 1 Cor. 1:27-29).
	3. The Lord appeared to Joshua prior to conquest activity (Josh. 5:13-6:5). 4. The ark of God had the central position when Israel crossed the Jordan (Josh. 3:6). 5. Joshua had to take the first step of faith, crossing the Jordan, before facing the Jericho challenge (Josh. 6:6-27). 6. The challenge to march against Ai immediately followed Israel's defeat there (Josh. 8). 7. The defeat of Jericho looked impossible, but God gave the victory (Josh 6). The defeat of Ai looked probable, but an initial attempt at conquest failed (Josh. 7).	3a. God will provide a leader with a foundation for the reasoning of faith. 3b. Great faith challenges will be accompanied by great moments of divine affirmation. 4a. Faith's focus mist be on the reality of God's abiding presence. 5a. Faith is ripened through successive challenges. 5b. One challenge will prepare a leader for greater challenges. 6a. A leader must not allow defeat to stop him/her from facing today's challenges. 6b. Defeat can have a debilitating effect. A faith challenge can reverse this effect. 7a. God is the one who gives the victory.
Flesh Acts	1. Joshua was deceived by the Gibeonites (Josh. 9:22).	1a. All things are not as they appear to be. 1b. Unusual stebacks must be explored for supernatural lessons. 1c. Obedience to God requires discernment and spiritual insight. 1d. A leader must depend upon God at all times because deceptive forces are at work to hinder God's purposes. 1e. "We not only need the power of God to overcome our obvious enemies, but also the wisdom of God to detect our subtle enemies" (Davis, 1988:78).
	2. Joshua's treaty with the Gibeonites, wrongly made, resulted in their inclusion in Israel life (Josh. 9).	2a. A flesh act can have corporate ramifications. 2b. Presumptuous faith (i.e. assuming God will do something that He has not comminicated to a leader) can lead to a flesh act. 2c. In major decisions, acting without consulting God often results in a flesh act. 2d. The difference between a faith challenge/flesh act is discernment of God's guidance. 2e. Alliances must be carefully analyzed for God's direction.
God's Word	1. God gave Joshua clear instructions regarding his involvement with the Book of the Law (Josh. 1:8). 2. In the midst of conquest, Joshua and the Israelites were found at Mount Ebal rehearsing the Book of the Law (Josh. 8:30-35). 3. Joshua wrote the Law on plastered stones for public display in the land (Josh. 3:8).	1a. God's Word is an important guidance and teaching factor for leaders (cf. Ps. 119:105). 1b. A leader's success is directly linked to his/her response to God's Word. 2a. Heeding God's Word is more crucial than fighting God's battles. 3a. A leader must communicate God's ways to the fullest extent of their influence. 3b. A leader has the responsibility to communicate God's principles to followers.

Chart 7 Table of Principles Phase III cont.

Name	Observation	Principle(s)
Guidance	1. God spoke to Joshua during crisis situations (Josh. 7; 10; 11). 2. When preparing to cross the Jordan River, Joshua merely told the people to prepare for the amazing thing God would do (Josh. 3:5, 6). 3. Joshua received specific instructions from God (Josh 3:8).	1a. A leader should expect God's specific guidance during crisis. 2a. While God's counsel may be revealed to a leader, often this counsel is communicated gradually. 3a. A leader must hear from God.
Leadership Transition	1. Joshua faced a significant faith challenge early in his sucession of Moses (Josh. 3). This challenge was followed by God's exaltation of him in the sight of Israel (Josh. 4:14). 2. Joshua received early assurance of God's continued presence (Josh. 1:9).	1a. In leadership transition of a high level leader, the spiritual authority of the new leader must be established early. 1b. In a God-directed leadership transition, the new leader can expect a spiritual authority experience which probably will involve a faith challenge, or some other significant item. 2a. Continuity supports successful transition.
Obedience	1. Joshua fully obeyed God by erecting a stone memorial at the Jordan River crossing. He also explained the significance of this act (Josh. 4). 2. The circumcision at Gilgal was necessary to roll away the reproach of Egypt (Josh. 5:9).	1a. Obedience often requires discernment. 1b. A mark of mture leadership is discernment of God's intent as well as His direction. 1c. Perceiving and communicating a course of action can do much to encourage the willful compliance of followers. 2a. Obedience is a key to entrance into God's promises.
Power	1. Joshua experienced the power of God's presence in the theophany (Josh. 5:13-15). 2. Achan's sin of covetousness stopped God's power for conquest. When sin was dealt with, victory came (Josh. 7).	1a. Power for leadership comes from God. 2a. Purity releases God's power.
Prayer Power	1. As a result of Joshua's praer, the sun and moon stood still, and the Israelites defeated their enemy (Josh. 10:12-14).	1a. Leadership is a cooperative effort with God. A leader must act, but God gives the victor in response to prayer. 1b. Answers to prayer will lend leadership credibility.
Sense of Destiny	1. God told Joshua, "You will lead these people to inherit the land I swore to their forefathers to give them" (Josh. 1:6). 2. God consistently revealed Himself to Joshua as the God who fought for Israel (Ex. 14:24, 25; 17:15; Josh. 5:13-6:5).	1a. A leader's destiny is linked to God's broader purposes. 1b. A leader is not an isolated individual, but a link in the network of God's timeless plan. 2a. God will provide a leader with the insights necessary to fulfill his/her calling. 2b. A leader should observe God's revelations to an emerging leader. These might be indicators of God's future design for the budding leader.
Sin	1. Because of Achan's sin, the people of Israel were charged with breaking faith, sinning, transgressing the covenant, taking, stealing, and lying (Josh. 7).	1a. The failure of one person affects the entire community of believers. 1b. Sin can cause the defeat and destruction of God's people. 1c. A leader must maintain the delicate network of interrelations among God's people. 1d. A leader's private actions, whether good or bad, affect the quality of corporate life. 1e. A leader is called to foster an environment of harmonious relationships that engender God's blessing. 1f. Sin can block the flow of divine power. 1g. Disobedience of a single follower to explicit commands, concerning a specific situation, can stop God's power for the entire body of believers. 1h. Selfishness will disintegrate community.
Spiritual Authority	1. After the Jordan River crossing, the Israelites revered Joshua all the days of his life (Josh. 4:14). 2. Joshua established a memorial commemorating God's intervention at the Jordan River. 3. When the Israelites were defeated at Ai, God spoke to Joshua, explained the reason for defeat, and told him what to do to correct the situation (Josh. 7).	1a. Supernatural demonstrations accompanying a leadership act will greatly affect the leader's power and right to influence. 1b. Spiritual authority, though conferred by people, is in the ultimate sense given (delegated) by God. 2a. Memorials can engender a faith-filled awe in a leader. 2b. Memorials proclaim God's acts and announce a leader's faith. 3a. The ability to hear God's voice, discern a situation, and lead God's people out of trouble will increase the depth of follower influence. 3b. A follower's false step, can become a leadership growth opportunity. 3c. God will back a leader who willingly places himself/herself under divine rules.

CONCLUSION
Reflections

At the beginning of this study a number of statements relating to interests and expectations were given. A reflection on these early anticipations is appropriate at this point.

Katherine.

My original interests in Joshua were sustained throughout this study. However, I discovered that my interest in the dynamics of spiritual warfare and faith took a back seat to the practical realities of character development. As the study progressed it became clear that successful spiritual warfare and the use of faith were dependent upon qualities such as obedience and courage, qualities forged in life's experiences (cf. Heb. 5:8). As a result, I've spent the first part of the conclusion emphasizing leadership beginnings.

My expectations regarding leadership development, leadership transition, and destiny fulfillment were met. In fact, these expectations were exceeded by some new discoveries in these areas. Related thoughts are conveyed in the following pages.

A Final Analysis

Joshua's life is a beautiful portrait of a leader. The distinctive elements of this pictorial tapestry are its three major strands: leadership development, leadership transition, and destiny fulfillment. Joshua's development was extensive. He spent at least forty-five years being trained to hit the divine target for his life. The leadership transition from Moses to Joshua was successful. And destiny fulfillment was many-faceted. Joshua was a key for initiating destiny fulfillment for a nation, for the patriarchs, and for himself. Thus, the development was gradual, the transition smooth, and the fulfillment broad.

The Beginning of Leadership

Are Leaders Born?

The question can be asked, "Are people born leaders, or do they learn to lead?" Clearly, some individual's have a greater probability of being successful at leadership. Some people, like Moses, seem to be born leaders. But this doesn't mean that leadership can't be learned, even by ordinary people. Douglas Hyde, a defected Communist Party leader, gave an interesting illustration on this point.

> Early in the last war I was conducting a leadership training course.... I ended my last lecture in this series by saying that the Communist Party could take anyone who was willing to be trained in leadership and turn him into a leader. I stepped down from the rostrum and there, awaiting me, was Jim.
>
> ...As I looked at him I thought that I had never seen anyone who looked less like a leader in my life....
>
> ...He was very short, grotesquely fat, with a flabby white face, a cast in one eye, and to make matters worse, a most distressing stutter.
>
> ...he came to me and said: C-c-c-comrade, I w-w-w-want you to-t-t-t-take me and t-t-t-turn me into a I-I-leader of m-m-m-men. 1 looked at Jim and wondered how I was going to do it (Hyde 1966:62).

Douglas undertook the task of leadership development and Jim became a successful national leader. It was Douglas' desire, as a renewed person, that Christians would get hold of this principle,

This illustration serves as a good backdrop for the Joshua story, It's not that Joshua resembles Jim in any physical way, but that God can take someone who is in the rough and transform him/her into a productive leader for His kingdom. Joshua began his life as a slave in Egypt, not a very noble beginning. He was a minority among the Egyptians, a social castaway. Later in life, as he stood alongside Moses, he must have keenly felt his own inadequacies. Moses was a leader "par excellence," how could Joshua ever measure up to such a model? And yet it was this man that God chose to play a significant role in Israel's national destiny.

Was Joshua born a leader, or did he learn leadership? I believe God called Joshua to be a leader. But the fact remains that the greater emphasis in his life was on leadership development. This is also the New Testament perspective. Qualifications for leadership in the pastoral epistles is based upon the degree of character development and not merely on giftedness (cf. I Tim. 3:1-13; Titus 1:6-9). In fact, giftedness seems to play a very minor role. So, while a person may be born a leader this may mean nothing if a process of leadership development does not take place. How Does a Leader Grow?

While many years are missing in the historical puzzle of growth, Joshua first emerged in scripture as a leader in training at forty-five years old. During this training season there were three major categories of learning opportunities: assignments or tasks; hardships; and people with whom Joshua came into contact (mentor and other relationships) (Kouzes and Posner, 1987:283). Each of these were important for growth and leadership education.

Joshua's development highlights the importance of learning through experience. There is no real substitute for learning by doing. The more chances a person has to serve in a leadership role, the more likely it is that he/she will learn important leadership tssons. *what il hate*

It's also helpful to have high visibility tasks. High visibility personally empowers an individual and aids advancement in the leadership network (Kouzes and Posner 1987:285). Joshua was placed in highly visible leadership tasks (Ex. 17:8-16 Nu. 13,14). These led to public acknowledgment of his skills. Opportunities like this moves a growing leader up the ladder of credibility, providing the job is done right.

Being part of a leadership team, or task force, can help a leader develop his/her ability to work with other people and groups. Joshua had been part of a leadership team. He had learned the value of other's giftedness, and the power of unified efforts (cf. Ex. 24:9-18). This was important when he had to motivate group activity for entrance into the Promised Land (Josh. 1:10-18).

Challenges were also crucial to Joshua's growth. "Challenge is the opportunity for greatness.... Leaders seek and accept challenging opportunities to test their abilities" (Kouzes and Posner 1987:29). A challenge is an opportunity for stretching leadership capacity. Skills emerge and hidden abilities are discovered. This is what happened to Joshua when the challenge of conquest was undertaken. A dimension of his character, previously not seen, shown forth. He is best known for his leadership during this challenging time frame, even though it was a very brief portion of his life.

Early hardships, both in the foundational and formational phase of Joshua's life taught him many lessons. Hardship forges character, gauges the level of development, and triggers self-insight. It's a learning tool and forging instrument fundamental to leadership growth.

People have always been an important source of growth and guidance to others. Relational influence is experienced throughout one's life.

Joshua had a key relationship with Moses that especially impacted his development. A powerful factor involved in a mentoring relationship such as Joshua's is expectation. Goodwin's expectation principle states that "a poten-

Can be seen in my life and imp. for Investing in others

tial leader tends to rise to the level of genuine expectancy of a leader he or she respects" (Clinton 1989:343). Expectations create a powerful motivating force for growth and formation.

> These expectations are powerful, because they...are frames into which people fit reality. In this way, you see what you expect to see, rather than what may be actually occurring. Social psychologists have referred to this as the Pygmalion effect, based on a Greek myth about Pygmalion, a sculptor who carved a statue of a beautiful woman, fell in love with the statue, and brought it to life by the strength of his perceptions (Kouzes and Posner 1987:242).

Moses played a Pygmalion-like role in developing Joshua. He believed in his protege. He promoted him, trusted him with responsibility, and saw him with prophetic eyes. Moses envisioned a future for the younger leader. He gave Joshua a new name reflecting that potential. The mentor's perceptions of Joshua were realized in the powerful environment of expectations.

Joshua's contact with other leaders taught him the importance of a leadership network. Leadership is not an isolated phenomenon. It is the result of successful interactions with others. Learning to relate well to other people is necessary for personal growth as well as professional advancement. On the professional level a network of relationships is important in accomplishing leadership.

The bottom line is that a growing leader will expand his/her base of experience. Learning from "observations based on experience...is a far better process for learning leadership than beginning with an a priori 'truth'" (Kouzes and Posner 1987:286). Opportunities for this type of advancement will be added to the leader's repertoire of qualifications. From this base, future leadership can take shape.

What Is Foundational for High Level Leadership?

Although processing is unique to each individual, Joshua's life reveals a key principle applicable to development in general. This principles is the servant principle found in Mark 10:43,44. Jesus said, "Whoever wants to become great among you must be your servant, and whoever wants to be first must be slave of all."

Joshua spent eighty-five years living and learning this principle. Although he had many roles throughout his life, during his foundational phase (in Egypt) he was a slave. A slave is a person bound in servitude (Gove 1981). In the formational phase (during the wilderness wanderings) he was a servant to Moses. A servant is one who is willingly submitted to servitude. Why so much emphasis on servanthood in Joshua's life? Because good followership qualities, are also good leadership qualities (Hollander 1978:6). God was developing a

Are they?

man who could handle responsibility and power, but at the same time remain responsive to the needs of the people just as a servant is responsive to his master. Servanthood is foundational for high-level leadership.

A Leadership Transition

Leadership transition is a complex process involving the old regime, the new regime, and a group of followers. A study of Joshua provides insight on how a leadership transition can be successfully implemented.

Where Does It All Begin?

God had long been grooming Joshua and preparing the Israelites for a shift in leadership. Leadership change did not happen overnight. A foundation was laid, prior to transition, that would allow a major shift in leadership to occur. Mentoring was a key in laying this foundation.

It's uncertain whether or not Moses had Joshua in mind as his successor before God spoke to him (Nu. 20:12). But the fact remains that Moses was careful to provide training for Joshua at a mentoring level. He also developed a leadership staff (cf. Ex. 24:,14; 2 Tim. 2:2). This created a strong leadership base. While Moses was the primary one in command, there were others who were able to assume key responsibilities. This must have created an environment of security, as well as receptivity to varying levels of leadership. The people were maturing as they learned to follow others.

Joshua's ongoing association with Moses at a mentoring level did at least two things. First, it promoted Joshua's development. Through tandem training Joshua was inculcating skills, attitudes and values needed for top level leadership. Second, it prepared the people for Joshua's installation. Whenever they saw Moses, Joshua was not far away. This gave Joshua credibility and created a positive perception of his status. "Leader legitimacy is related to having as an influence source" (Hollander 1978:52). Leadership legitimacy was being established. Opportunities for successes in assigned tasks added leadership competence to legitimacy. By the time Joshua was chosen as Moses' successor, he had gained credits from earlier activities. The overall effect of tandem training was to create a sense of trust and ease among followers. When Joshua would assume the primary position, these past interactions would lend stability to his leadership.

How Is the Right Leader Selected?

The first step in the selection process is a realization by the older leader that it's time to step down. Moses knew his job was finished and the time had come to find a replacement (Nu. 27:15-17). At this point, he didn't call together a council or take votes. He prayed and asked for God's choice. God responded with the selection of Joshua.

Too often leadership selection is not a prime prayer concern. While education and experiential qualifications are important, the determining consideration should be God's word, "This is my chosen one." Samuel would not have selected David as the future king had he based his decision on outward appearances (I Sam. 16:1-13). He would have chosen Eliab (v.6). But God straightened Samuel out by giving him the divine selection criterion, "Do not consider his appearance or his height, for I have rejected him. The Lord does not look at the things man look at. Man looks at the outward apearance, but the Lord looks at the heart" (v.7). Had Samuel gone by his natural instincts, he would have chosen the wrong person. In the New Testament, Barnabas and Saul were selected and catapulted into their life's work because God chose them (Acts13:1-3). Had the disciples not placed themselves in a position to hear from God, Paul might never have been initiated into ministry, and half of our New Testament might never have been written. When the selection is directed and empowered by God, transition is off to a successful start.

What Can Be Done to Ease Leadership Transition?

After selecting Joshua as his successor, Moses appointed him in a public leadership act (Nu. 27:18-23). There was a definite leadership selection. Moses left no room for questions concerning Joshua's appointment, no ambiguities or scrambles for the top position after his death. He settled it ahead of time, giving a public ceremony with his backing. He did what he could to remove uncertainty about the future (Deut. 3:21-29; 31). The change occurred in the open. The steps to be taken were clearly articulated.

> Uncertainty reduction is an important benefit the leader provides....a significant need in most human activity is to limit, or at least to minimize uncertainty....where it is present it often acts to immobilize people, whether individually or collectively. Prolonged uncertainty, especially about a matter of importance, can produce anxiety which causes a breakdown in normal functioning.... (Hollander 1978:10,11).

Moses was concerned with uncertainty reduction. Whether or not he knew the implications of all that he was doing, his actions helped to minimize the breakdown of normal activity and to provide emotional stability. He clearly stated God's choice of Joshua as his successor. The baton was being passed. The task of bringing the Israelites into the promised land was publicly given to Joshua.

Moses provided further assurance of continuity (Deut. 31:2-8). He told the Israelites, "The same God who dealt with Sihon and Og, will deal with the men across the river" (v.4). Then turning to Joshua he essentially said, 'The same God who has been with me will go before you. Don't be afraid" As a keen leader, Moses firmly established the continuity of Yahweh's supernatural leadership, a leadership that had been constant since the time of Abraham (Schaeffer 1975:39). Assurance of God's continued leadership provided certainty in the midst of change.

Moses was also wise enough to recognize, and make provision for, Joshua's limitations. When transitioning him into leadership, he saw that Joshua was a charismatic, militaristic leader, but not necessarily the spiritual leader at this point. Thus, he set Eleazar into this spiritual role, publicly bolstering him in the eyes of the people (Nu. 27:21). In doing this, Moses was compensating for Joshua's weaknesses, and assuring the installment of a functional system. A successful transition will consider the current and future needs of the new leader.

A new leader following an older leader must not look back and compare. One way to overcome this tendency is to have a big challenge, a new task not done by the former leader. Joshua was given such a task, the conquest and establishment of Canaan. This task was significant enough to direct Joshua's attention toward the future, and to help the people identify him with a contribution that was uniquely his own. Thus, Joshua was able to stand on his own merit and not merely the merit of another.

Moses had done a lot in placing Joshua into his new role, but Joshua needed personal assurance of God's appointment. This assurance was given in Deuteronomy 31:14-18 and Joshua 1. God spoke directly to Joshua concerning this appointment. Another personal word from the Lord promised public affirmation. The Lord told Joshua, "Today I will begin to exalt you in the eyes of all Israel, so they may know that I am with you as I was with Moses" (Josh. 3:7). This word was fulfilled on that day (Josh. 4:14). A leader in transition needs a personal sense of God's approval both privately and publicly.

Finally, an early leadership success landed Joshua safely on the other side of transition. The Lord's gave him a tactical plan for the defeat of Jericho (Josh. 5:13-6:5). The result: an overwhelming success. This early success stimulated confidence in Joshua and his followers. With it came assurance and closure to the transition experience.

How Does Leadership Transition affect Followers?

Transition is a major change at the organizational level affecting many people in varying degrees. During change mixed feelings are unleashed, some positive and some negative. For example, in the wilderness, the Israelites had responded to their geographical change in negative ways (cf. Ex. 15:22-27; 16; 17:1-7). A common complaint had been, "Why did you bring us out of Egypt (Ex. 17:3). On the other hand, the new generation of Israelites accepted the changes that later took place. They willingly embraced Joshua's new leadership (Josh. 1:16-18) and followed him without the common grumbling associated with their parents. Why the difference? Tichy and Ulrich may provide us with some hints.

According to Tichy and Ulrich transition involves a three-phase process of individual change: first come endings, followed by neutral zones, and then new beginnings (1984:65-66). All transitions begin with endings. In the Moses/Joshua transition the ending of Moses' leadership was signaled when Moses was denied access into the Promised Land (Nu. 20:12) and initiated when God chose Joshua to succeed him (Nu. 27:12-17).

The first task in the *ending phase* is to *disengage* (1984:65). This often involves a physical transaction. When coming out of Egypt the Israelites disengaged. There was a physical transfer from one place to another. In publicly commissioning Joshua, Moses was helping the next generation of Israelites to disengage. Joshua's commissioning was a tangible act that enabled the people to transfer their loyalties and disengage from the old regime.

The second task in the ending phase is to *disidentify* (1984:65). This was probably not too difficult for the Israelites because their identity was not centered in an individual) as much as it was in their Lord. Their identity was wrapped up in Yahweh. That's probably why there was so much emphasis on God's promise, presence, word, and people during the time immediately following Moses' death (cf. Josh. 1).

The third task in this phase is *disenchantment* (1984:65). Disenchantment is the recognition that past situations will not be possible to replicate in the future. This seems to be where the wilderness Israelites failed. They remained attached to sentiments, as erroneous as they may have been, of the "good old days" (Ex. 17:3). On the other hand, during the Moses/Joshua transition the people focused on new circumstances. They weren't enchanted by the past, but by the future. They were focused on what lay ahead. The past was behind them. The task of conquest captivated their imaginations.

The second phase in a transition process is the *neutral zone*. This is a "time out" period in which people adjust to change. It is a time of "reorientation where individuals complete endings and begin new patterns of behavior" (Tichy and Ulrich 1984:66). The wilderness generation never entered this phase. These Israelites dropped out of the transition process before reaching this point. In contrast, the new generation of Israelites had a neutral zone experience. During the major leadership transition, there was an indefinite period of time between Joshua's selection as successor and Moses' death. It was a period of leadership overlap, a neutral time which gave the Israelites an opportunity to adjust to the change.

The final phase is *new beginnings*. After going through the previous processing people can continue in a forward direction with new enthusiasm and commitment. This enthusiasm and commitment was demonstrated by the Israelites' response to Joshua, "Whatever you have commanded us we will do, and wherever you send us we will go" (Josh. 1:16). Thus, a major change occurred as the Israelites passed through transition.

DESTINY FULFILLMENT
Reaching Personal and Corporate Goals

Everyone Has a Destiny

Every person and every Christian organization has an ultimate goal, a target God intends for them to hit. Paul said, "I press on toward the goal to win the prize for which God has called me heavenward in Christ Jesus" (Phil. 3:14). Paul had an ultimate goal to achieve, a personal destiny to fulfill. He obtained that goal and won his prize (2 Tim. 4:6-8).

Isaiah 49:1-2 describes Jesus as a polished arrow. The purpose of an arrow is to hit a target. That target is the divine goal for one's life. The purpose of the Lamb of God was to hit the mark, the cross. Satan offered Jesus every inducement in order to deflect Him from that mark. But Jesus resolutely headed for Jerusalem where the cross awaited Him (Lk. 9:51). He was determined not to be detoured. He had a destiny to fulfill. He hit the target and became the Savior of the world.

Joshua had a goal for his life, a goal established and ordained by God. Its parameters were outlined by Moses and direct revelation from the Lord. Joshua 11:15 declares that he completed his task and reached his goal: "As the Lord commanded his servant Moses, so Moses commanded Joshua, and Joshua did it; he left nothing undone of all that the Lord commanded Moses." As an arrow Joshua hit the target, his ultimate destiny.

There is a mark for everyone to hit and a time appointed by God in which the arrow is shot forth by the Holy Spirit to hit that mark. Whether or not one hits the mark depends upon a realization of God's intentions, and upon the all-important preparation time in which character is formed and refined.

Ultimate Goals Are God-Given

The first thing that's clear in Joshua's life is the origin of his destiny. It was God who called him, prepared him, and revealed the divine intentions for his life. While these intentions unfolded over a lifetime, they guided his steps along the way. Goal clarification must come from God, but it is often a gradual process of progressive revelation. But Joshua didn't get ahead of the Lord. He lived according to the level of revealed expectations.

As a destiny leader, Joshua had come to an understanding of God's personal and corporate direction. The divine intention had become firmly fixed in his vision. It's essential for leaders to come to a clear understanding of God's personal and corporate destinies. As a nation, Israel was birthed in the heart of God. Israel was His idea. God outlined her destiny and plotted her course. One of her divinely inspired goals was the acquisition of God's land inheritance - Canaan. This was God's idea. Joshua's leadership was God's idea. God had prepared him and moved him into position. God confimed him and affirmed his leadership.

One's ultimate goal must be the goal God envisions. The responsibility of plotting one's course of life must begin with an understanding of God's direction. Again, destiny revelation is progressive; thus the requirement is to walk according to the level of divine revelation available at that time.

This is so important in destiny fulfillment. A person has to be on the right track in order to reach their destination. There are many things an individual, or organization can do, many good things. Many wonderful things. But are they God's "things"? Whatever Joshua did, he did because God directed him. He was successful in the battle against Jericho. Why? Because God told him to go there. God told him what to do. Goal clarification through divine revelation is a must. This is the essence of destiny revelation.

A minister once shared a story about his grandfather's tomato plants. His grandfather had many tomatoes in his garden. However, some of the plants didn't do as well as others. One plant in particular had an unusually thick stem. Oddly enough it only produced small tomatoes. What a contrast it was to the rest of them. The others had thin, wispy vines bearing large tomatoes. Grandfather had a good explanation. The thick stemmed plant was using most of its nutrients to support the stem, But the thinner ones weren't. They were channelling most of their nutrients into the fruit, producing a wonderful harvest.

This illustration can be compared to a leader or Christian organization. If a person does not understand God's goal for his/her life, he/she can become involved in many activities but never really accomplish what God intends. The life of the spirit is used up on things that aren't necessary. Not much fruit is produced for the Kingdom of God. The same holds true for a group. Joshua could have randomly decided to return to Egypt and overthrow Pharaoh. What good would that have done? Would it have accomplished God's purposes for Israel? No, it would have made Israel a "fat stem" but not a fruitful one. God didn't need Pharaoh or any additional land for His purposes. One author put it so well when he said that his greatest fear is that he would succeed at something God had not called him to do. Joshua's direction, goal, and destiny came from God.

Faith, Obedience and Courage Are Keys to Obtaining God's Goals

Once Joshua understood his destiny, how did he move into destiny fulfillment? Following are a few points gleaned from this study.

In reviewing Joshua's life the three main process items that emerged were the faith challenge, mentoring, and spiritual authority discovery. This is an interesting combination because many commentators agree that the key qualities Joshua needed to enter into destiny fulfillment were faith, obedience, and courage. This is born out in scripture. Joshua had been given God's promises (Josh. 1:3,4,5). His responsive actions were the language of faith. A serious exhortation to obedience was given (Josh. 1:7-8). And at least three times God exhorted him to be courageous. Faith challenges tested and developed Joshua's faith. Mentoring had taught him careful obedience. And spiritual authority discoveries engendered courage based on an awareness of the divine source of his leadership rights.

God will prepare a leader with the adequate training necessary to accomplish his/her life's work. While this training will vary according to one's calling, it seems safe to conclude that there are three necessary ingredients for entering into, and obtaining one's destiny. These ingredients are faith, obedience and courage.

Faith is necessary for accomplishing God's goals. Hebrews 11:6 says, "Without faith it is impossible to please God." The accomplishments of the people in this chapter of Hebrews were the result of faith. By faith the walls of Jericho fell down (Heb. 11:30). Joshua took action in battle based on his belief that God's word was true in spite of evidence to the contrary. Once a person understand's God's direction, faith is needed to follow through. Entering into destiny fulfillment will require the action of a living, vital faith. God will give prior opportunities for its development and exercise.

Obedience was an important key in Joshua's destiny. His ultimate testimony in Joshua 11:15 verifies this fact: "He left nothing undone of all that the Lord commanded Moses." Entrance into one's destiny requires unqualified obedience. God can't lead a person to their divinely ordained goal, if they don't follow. Joshua learned how to be a good follower in his relationship with Moses. As a former slave and servant he knew what it meant to do the bidding of another. For years he had functioned in a role that required an attitude which says, "Not my will, but your's be done." A leader should willingly adopt a submissive posture to the influence of older leaders (cf. I Peter. 5:5). A pattern of obedience will develop which will be useful in future ministry.

Jesus fulfilled his destiny in the same way. He told the pharisees, "I do nothing on my own but speak just what the Father has taught me" (John.

8:2829). Jesus acted, not on His own initiative, but on the initiative of His Father. Unqualified obedience led Him to the cross and to His ultimate testimony (Mt. 24:42). Why is obedience so necessary? Because God knows the plan and the way for obtaining the divine objective. Because He knows what's going on "behind the scenes" and His strategy will take this into account. Because it's His desire that He receive all the glory (cf I Cor. 131).

Courage will strengthen faith in the face of overwhelming obstacles. Joshua needed courage to follow in the footsteps of Moses as well as courage for conquest. Every leader will face situations requiring courage to overcome obstacles. This is particularly true when taking the initial steps toward one's goal, especially if that goal is full-time ministry. Spiritual authority discovery will build a confidence base for leadership. Courage comes from the Lion of the Tribe of Judah. Unique times with Him will become the source of this quality.

Memorials Mark Progress Toward Goal Fulfillment

A "memorial or remembering in Hebrew is more than a recalling to mind. It involves remembering with concern; it also implies loving reflection and then action" (Hughes 1987:56).

One purpose of a memorial is to provide a destiny reminder. Biblical memorials were marks of God's historical involvement with His people. But they marked significant elements of His involvement, those elements that were keys in their progress toward His purposes. Thus, memorials were destiny reminders, reminders of a destiny intimately linked to Yahweh. They served to kindle a loving reflection on the God who was directing His people. These reflections were intended to stir to current action. For example, the Passover celebration was a destiny marker signifying God's deliverance from Egypt. If God could take this step in fulfilling Israel's destiny, couldn't He continue to lead the Israelites into their inheritance? Couldn't He part the waters of Jordan that stood between them and the Promised Land? A memorial says, "If He did it before, He can do it again." It is a tangible testimonial of God's commitment to the destiny of His people.

A brief look at Israelite history reveals a series of memorials, each signifying a significant moment in their national destiny. The Passover marked God's deliverance and intention to fulfill His promise of a land inheritance (Ex. 12:14). The manna samples reminded the Israelites of God's provision and faithfulness to lead them through a difficult phase of destiny fulfillment. The twin pile of stones in the Jordan and at Gilgal reminded of God's power, and marked a significant destiny step (Josh .4). The pile of stones in Trouble Valley testified to the power of sin to hinder their destiny as the people of God (Josh. 7:26). The altar on Mount Ebal reminded them of their relationship with God which defined their destiny (Josh. 8:30). And the monumental stone with God's word written on it was a statement of the quality of life that sustained their destiny. Each of these memorials united the Israelites' around Yahweh and created a sense of corporate purpose and cohesiveness, important elements in moving an organization toward its goals.

Establishing memorials is important in destiny fulfillment and goal attainment. This is especially true on the corporate level. Moving a group into God's purposes requires a unified effort. Memorials encourage slacking members and unify the organizational vision around God's goals. They also help to define these goals. Memorials thus become a means of institutionalizing a corporate destiny so that it's vision lasts over the long haul of time.

There Are Hindrances to Destiny Fulfillment

Personal and corporate destinies can be hindered. A main hindrance is sin. In Joshua 7, Achan's sin stopped the flow of God's power and Israel's progression into God's promise. Personal and corporate holiness must be maintained. This means that a leader must watch his/her life closely (1 Tim. 4:16), and take steps to safeguard organizational wholeness.

Another hindrance is failure to secure divine guidance, particularly in major decisions. Because Joshua didn't seek the Lord concerning a treaty with the Gibeonites, he inadvertently disobeyed God's instructions (Josh. 9). This opened the door for an idolatrous community to become a part of Israel's's national life.

God is the one who guides a person into his/her destiny. This requires ongoing sensitivity to His direction and specific inquiry over larger issues. Abraham might never have given birth to Ishmael had he listened to God. It was Ishmael's descendants who opposed God's people in subsequent years. This lad's seed became Israel's "thorn in the flesh. Sin, and failure to inquire of the Lord, will hamper destiny fulfillment.

Finally, a word of caution. A danger in reaching one's goal is complacency. While Joshua remained steadfast in the Lord, Israel's apostasy began after she entered the land. According to Hosea 11:12, no sooner is the "son" in the land than the covenant relationship with Yahweh is broken. While apostasy may occur, it's more likely that complacency will create a plateau barrier (Clinton 1989:177). The barrier is complacency, becoming comfortable with the way things are. A goal has been reached, a significant portion of one's destiny attained; so why move on? This attitude will hinder further growth and progression toward the completion of God's purpose. A plateau of false satisfaction is reached and forward movement stops. A leader in this position never enters into ministry completion. God's full intention for his/her life may bud, but does not blossom.

APPENDIX A

Glossary of Terms

AFTERGLOW PHASE. A term used to label the sixth development phase of a leader's life. Synonym: Celebration.

AUTHORITY INSIGHT PROCESS ITEM - P(AI). Refers to those instances in ministry in which a leader learns important lessons, via positive or negative experiences, with regards to 1) submission to authority, 2) authority structures, 3) authenticity of power bases underlying authority, 4) authority conflict, 5) how to exercise authority.

BASIC SKILLS PROCESS ITEM - P(BS). Refers to actual skills acquired and/or values learned in picking up those skills, during the foundational phase, which will later affect leadership skills, leadership attitudes, and leadership styles.

BOUNDARY. The label given to the time immediately preceding the end of a sub-phase or phase which usually is made up of an entry stage, transition stage, and termination stage.

COMPETENT AUTHORITY. The form of power in which a leader obtains or can expect (but not demand) compliance by virtue of acknowledged expertise in some field of endeavor. The authority is limited to that field of endeavor.

CONTEXTUAL PROCESS ITEMS - P(CXT). Those providential factors arising in local, regional, national, and international situations during a leader's life-history which affect spiritual, ministerial, and strategic formations, and frequently give God's strategic guidance for the leader.

CONVERGENCE. The condition of ministry for an idealized development, i.e, the development of a leader who has matured in leadership character, leadership skills, and leadership values.

CRISIS PROCESS ITEM - P(CR). Those special intense situations of pressure in human situations which are use by God to test and teach dependence.

DESTINY FULFILLMENT PROCESS ITEM -P(DF). Describes a grouping of process items which are significant acts, people, providential circumstances, or timing which represent the completion of destiny processing that has gone on previously.

DESTINY PREPARATION PROCESS ITEM - P(DP). Describes a grouping of process items concerning significant acts, people, providential circumstances, or timing, which hint at some future or special significance to a life and, when studied in retrospect, add firmness to a growing awareness of sense of destiny in a leader's life.

DESTINY REVELATION/CONFIRMATION - P(DR). Describes a grouping of incidents or process items with an unusual sense of God's presence working in them, and which are significant acts, people, providential circumstances, or timing which confirm a future destiny and perhaps begin to clarify its nature.

DEVELOPMENT PHASE. A marked off length on a time-line representing a significant portion of time in a leader's life history in which notable development takes place usually following a repetitive standard development pattern.

DEVELOPMENT TASK. Refers to the general and unique goals of a development phase and to which processing in the phase is directed.

DIVINE AFFIRMATION PROCESS ITEM - P(DA). A special kind of sense of destiny experience in which God gives approval to a leader so that the leader has a renewed sense of ultimate purpose and a refreshed desire to continue serving God.

DOUBLE CONFIRMATION PROCESS ITEM - P(DBLC). Refers to the unusual guidance process item in which God makes clear His will by giving the guidance directly to a leader and then reinforcing it by some other person totally independent and unaware of the leader's guidance.

ENTRY CONTEXT PROCESS ITEM - P(EC). Refers to those items related to the setting, both culturally and historically, of the local, regional, national, and international situation into which a leader is born and will minister in and which will be used by God to process a leader in terms of strategic guidance, long term convergence, and sense of destiny.

FAITH CHALLENGE PROCESS ITEM - P(FCHG). Refers to those instances in ministry where a leader is challenged to take steps of faith in regards to ministry and sees God meet those steps of faith with divine affirmation and ministry achievement in such a way as to increase the leader's capacity to trust God in future ministry.

FAMILY INFLUENCE PROCESS ITEM - P(FI). Refers to significant situations, events, and personalities that occurred in the early family life of a leader which helped mold character, perspectives, abilities, etc. of the person and which play a significant part in God's later leadership intentions.

FLESH ACT PROCESS ITEM - P(FLESH). Refers to those instances in a leader's life where guidance is presumed and decisions are made either hastily or without proper discernment of God's choice. Such decisions usually involve the working out of guidance by the leader using some human manipulation or other means andwhich brings ramifications which later negatively affect ministry and life.

IDEAL ROLE DISCOVERY PROCESS ITEM - P(IRD). Refers to any significant discovery or use of a role which enhances a leader's giftedness and maximizes influence-mix effectiveness.

IDEAL INFLUENCE-MIX DISCOVERY PROCESS ITEM - P(IMD). Refers to any significant discovery or use of the combination of influence-mix which results from harmonizing of major and minor convergence factors.

INFLUENCE-MIX. A term describing the combination of influence elements - direct, indirect or organizational - in terms of degree and kind at a given point in time.

ISOLATION PROCESS ITEM - P(I). Refers to the setting aside of a leader from normal ministry involvement in its natural context usually for an extended time in order to experience God in a new or deeper way.

LEADER. A person with a God-given capacity and with God-given responsibility who is influencing a specific group of God's people toward God's purposes for the group.

LEADERSHIP BACKLASH PROCESS ITEM - P(LB). Refers to the reactions of followers, other leaders within a group, and/or Christians outside the group, to a course of action taken by a leader because of various ramifications that arise due to the action taken. The situation is used in the leader's life to test perseverance, clarity of vision, and faith.

LEADERSHIP COMMITTAL - P(LCOM). Is a destiny process item, either an event or process which culminates in an acknowledgment from a potential leader to God of willingness to be used in ministry in whatever way God indicates.

LEADERSHIP RELEASE. The process whereby an existing leader deliberately encourages and allows an emerging leader to accept responsibility for and control of leadership positions, functions, roles and tasks.

LEADERSHIP TRANSITION. The process whereby existing leaders prepare and release emerging leaders into the responsibility and practice of leadership positions, functions, roles, and tasks.

LEGITIMATE AUTHORITY. The form of power in which a leader obtains compliance by using influence pressure consonant with common expectations of the role or positions held by the follower and leader.

LITERARY PROCESS ITEM - P(LI). Refers to the means whereby God is able to teach leaders lessons for their own lives through the writings of others.

MENTOR. A term in leadership development theory that refers to a leader who, at an opportune moment, facilitates, in any one of a variety of ways, the development of an emergent leader toward realization of potential.

MENTORING PROCESS ITEM - P(M). Refers to the process where a person with a serving, giving, encouraging attitude (the mentor) sees leadership potential in a still-to-be developed person (the protege) and is able to promote or otherwise significantly influence the protege along to the realization of potential.

MINISTERIAL FORMATIONS. Refers to that development of a leader which relates to effective leadership - the capacity to influence followers and to minister to them. It refers to development of ministry skills and knowledge.

MINISTRY AFFIRMATION PROCESS ITEM - P(MAF). A special kind of destiny experience in which God gives approval to a leader in terms of some ministry assignment in particular or some ministry experience in general which results in a renewed sense of purpose for the leader.

MINISTRY PHILOSOPHY. Refers to ideas, values, and principles whether implicit or explicit which a leader uses as guidelines for decision making, for exercising influence, and for evaluating his/her ministry.

MINISTRY STRUCTURAL INSIGHT - P(MSI). Refers to those discoveries about the various organizational units through which ministry is channelled and the effects of those discoveries on leadership capacity.

MINISTRY TASK PROCESS ITEM - P(MT). An assignment from God which primarily tests a person's faithfulness and obedience but often also allows use of ministry gifts in the context of a task which has closure, accountability, and evaluation.

NEGATIVE PREPARATION PROCESS ITEM - P(NEG). Refers to the special processing which involves God's use of events, people, conflict, persecution, or experiences, and which focus on the negative, in order to free up a person from the situation in order to enter the next phase of development with a new abandonment and revitalized interest.

NETWORKING POWER PROCESS ITEM - P(NP). The unusual use by God of mentors, divine contacts, or other related leaders, to channel power in order to open doors to accomplish influence goals far a leader so that the leader senses the importance of relationships with other leaders and knows the touch of God through networks of people.

OBEDIENCE CHECK PROCESS ITEM - P(OC). Refers to that special category of process items in which God tests personal response to revealed truth in the life of a person.

OVERLAP. That unique time in a leadership transition when the emerging leader and existing leader share responsibility and accountability for direct and indirect ministry functions of a leadership position.

PIVOTAL POINTS. Refers to a critical process item, or perhaps series of items, which curtail further use or expansion of the leader, limit the eventual use of the leader for ultimate purposes, or enhances and opens up the leader for expansion or contribution toward ultimate purposes in God's Kingdom.

POWER BASE. Refers to the source of credibility, power differential, or resources which enables a leader (power holder) to have authority to exercise influence on followers (power subjects).

POWER PROCESS ITEM - P(POWER). Refers to those demonstrations of God's intervention which convinces followers that God is indeed supporting the leader in the ministry for which the leader is responsible.

POWER-MIX. A term describing the combination of power forms - force, manipulation, authority, persuasion - which dominate a leader's influence in leadership acts during a given point of time in a development phase.

PRAYER CHALLENGE PROCESS ITEM - P(PC). Refers to those instances in ministry where God, in an unusual way impresses a leader with the essential spiritual dynamic lesson of ministry - a leader in ministry must pray for that ministry - and in which there is positive growth that will affect later ministry.

PRAYER POWER PROCESS ITEM - P(PP). Refers to the specific instance of the use of specific prayer to meet a situation in such a way that it is clear that God has answered the prayer and demonstrated the authenticity of the leader's spiritual authority.

PROCESS INCIDENTS. Refers to the actual occurrences from a given life of those providential events, people, circumstances, special divine interventions, inner-life lessons, and/or other like items which God uses to develop that person by shaping leadership character, leadership skills, and leadership values so as to indicate leadership capacity, expand potential, confirm appointment to roles, and direct that leader along God's appointed ministry level for realized potential.

PROCESS ITEM. Refers to a label inductively drawn from a comparative analysis of process incidents which categorizes incidents into groups with like properties.

RELATIONAL INSIGHT PROCESS ITEM - P(RI). Refer to those instances in ministry in which a leader learns lessons via positive or negative experiences with regard to relating to other Christians or non-Christians in the light of ministry decisions or other influence means; such lessons are learned so as to significantly affect future leadership.

SENSE OF DESTINY. An inner conviction arising from an experience or a series of experiences (in which there is a growing sense of awareness in retrospective analysis of those experiences) that God has His hand on a leader in a special way for special purposes.

SPHERE OF INFLUENCE. Refers to the totality of people being influenced and for whom a leader will give an account to God.

SPIRITUAL AUTHORITY. That characteristic of a God-anointed leader developed upon an experiential power base which enables a leader to influence followers through persuasion, force of modeling and moral expertise toward God's purposes.

SPIRITUAL AUTHORITY DISCOVER PROCESS ITEM - P(SAD). Refers to any significant discovery, insight, or experience, which advances a leader along the spiritual authority development pattern.

SUB-PHASE. A marked off length on a time-line within a development phase which points out an intermediate time of development during the development phase.

TANDEM TRANSITION TRAINING. A training technique used by an existing leader with an emerging leader in which the younger leader shares the learning experiences of the older via modeling, mentoring, apprenticeship, or internships so as to leapfrog the younger leader's development.

WORD CHECK PROCESS ITEM - P(WC). A process item which tests a leader's ability to understand or receive a word from God personally and to see it worked out in life with a view toward enhancing the authority of God's truth and a desire to know it.

WORD PROCESS ITEM - P(WI). An instance in which a leader receives a word from God which affects significantly a leader's guidance, committal, decision making, personal value system, spiritual formation, spiritual authority , or ministry philosophy.

APPENDIX B
Direct Biblical Data on Joshua

Following is a list of biblical incidences with direct reference to Joshua.

This list is not exhaustive, but covers the main events in Joshua's life. Also included is the major process item for each event.

Exodus 17:8-16 - Battle at Rephidim - Ministry Task
Exodus 24:9-18 - Alone for Forty Days on Mount Sinai - Spiritual Authority Discovery
Exodus 32:15-35 - Joshua With Moses When Confronting Idolatry - Authority Insight
Exodus 33:7-11 - Joshua In the Tent of Meeting With God- Spiritual Authority Discovery
Numbers 11:24-30 - Joshua Bothered By Prophesying Leaders - Relationship Insight
Numbers 13,14 - Spying Out the Land and Opposition - Faith Challenge

Numbers 27:12-23 - Selection of Joshua As Moses Successor - Leadership Committal
Deuteronomy 3:21-29 - Moses' Speech Mentioning Joshua - Destiny Revelation
Deuteronomy 31 - Joshua's Commissioning - Leadership Committal
Deuteronomy 34 - Succeeding an Awesome Leader - Faith Challenge

Joshua 1 - God's Charge - Destiny Revelation
Joshua 2 - Spying Out Jericho - Divine Affirmation
Joshua 3 - Crossing the Jordan - Faith Challenge
Joshua 4 - Establishing Memorials of Israel's Jordan Crossing - Divine Affirmation
Joshua 5:1-12 - Circumcision of Israel's Men - Obedience Check

Joshua 5:13-6:5 - Encounter With the Lord of Hosts - Spiritual Authority Discovery
Joshua 6:5-27 - Jericho Conquered - Faith Challenge
Joshua 7 - Dealing With Achan's Sin - Relationship Insight
Joshua 8:1-29 - Defeat of Ai - Faith Challenge
Joshua 8:30-35 - Reading God's Law on Mount Ebal - Literary Item
Joshua 9 - Deception By the Gibeonites - Flesh Act
Joshua 10 - Conquest Over the Southern Cities - Ministry Affirmation
Joshua 11 - Conquest Over the Northern Kings - Ministry Affirmation
Joshua 12 - A Recap of the Defeated Kings - Ministry Affirmation

Joshua 13-22 - Dividing the Land and Establishing a New Society -
        Ideal Role Discovery

Joshua 23,24 - Joshua's Final Days/Speeches - Destiny Fulfillment

APPENDIX C

Comparisons Between Joshua and Moses

There were many similarities between Joshua and Moses. These similarities are likely reflections of Moses' mentoring influence upon Joshua. They include, but are not restricted to, the following:

1. God was with Joshua as he was with Moses (cf. Josh. 1:5;3:7; Ex. 14:31).

2. The people pledged to obey Joshua as they did Moses (Josh. 1:17),

3. Both sent spies into the Promised Land (cf. Josh. 2:1; Nu. 13).

4. Both crossed the water miraculously (cf. Josh. 3:17; Ex. 14:26-31).

5. People revered Joshua as they had revered Moses (Josh. 4:14).

6. Joshua set up a twelve stone memorial (Josh. 4:5). Moses set up twelve pillars around an altar at the Sinai covenant ceremony (Ex. 24:14).

7. Joshua was required to circumcise the Israelites before entering Canaan (Josh. 5:1-12). God required that Moses' son be circumcised before delivering Israel (Ex. 4:24-26).

8. Both had a "burning bush" experience (cf. Josh. 5:15; Ex. 3:5).

9. Both interceded for the sinning Israelites (cf. Josh. 7:7; Deut. 9:25-29 and Nu. 14:13-19).

10. Joshua help up his javelin until victory was won at Ai (Josh. 8:18,26). Moses held up his hands until victory was won at Rephidim (Ex. 17:11-13).

11. Both wrote the law on stones (cf. Josh. 8:3% Ex. 24:12).

12. Both read curses and blessings from Mount Ebal (cf. Josh. 8:30-35; Deut. 27:28).

13. God hardened the hearts of both of their enemies (cf. Josh. 11:2& Ex. 9:12).

14. The Bible links Eleazar with Joshua as it did Moses with Aaron (cf. Nu. 27:19-21; Ex. 4:13-17).

15. At the end of their life's work both delivered stirring addresses of warning and appeal to the Israelites (cf. Josh. 24; Deut. 31,32).

APPENDIX D

The Moses/Joshua Model of Leadership Transition

Leadership transition is the process whereby existing leaders prepare and release emerging leaders into the responsibility and practice of leadership positions, functions, roles, and tasks. The process is best understood when viewed along a continuum as seen in Chart 8.

Replacement of Leader			Replacement of Leadership		
the leader's role	major responsibility for functions	pick up some functions	role with many tasks	more or complicated task(s)	simple task
Practicing Leader increasingly RELEASES					
Emerging Leader increasingly accepts RESPONSIBILITY					

Chart 8. The Leadership Transition Continuum

On the left is the maximum limit of leadership transition - that is, the leader him/herself is replaced totally from the leadership situation. The emerging leader thus becomes the new leader and is totally responsible for the leadership situation. On the right is the minimum, the present leader turns over some small piece of leadership - a simple task. A task is an observable assignment of usually short duration. As one moves across the continuum faithful performance of simple tasks leads to increasing responsibility such as a role. A role is a recognizable position which does a major portion of the ministry. It probably has several on-going tasks associated with it. Faithful or successful accomplishment of a role will lead to greater responsibility - usually wider roles and responsibility for important functions of the ministry as a whole. Leadership functions is a technical term which refers to the three major categories of formal leadership responsibility: task behavior (defining structure and goals), relationship behavior (providing the emotional support), and inspirational behavior (providing motivational effort). Each of these major leadership functions has several specific sub-functions.

In between, various levels of transition are experienced As you move from right to left on the continuum, the present leader is increasingly releasing more tasks, functions and finally major responsibility for the ministry. Leadership release is the process whereby an existing leader deliberately encourages and allows an emerging leader to accept responsibility for and control of leadership positions, functions, roles, and tasks. This is signified by the arrow moving toward the left. The function of release is a difficult one for most leaders. The tendency is to either over-control on the one hand (authoritarian defensive posture), or to give too much responsibility without adequate supervision or transitional training on the other (the quick release posture). The first tendency tends to suffocate emerging leaders and frustrate them. Such a posture usually drives them out to another ministry where they can be released. The second tendency overwhelms them and usually insures failure in their first attempt at leadership. This can be discouraging and cause some to decide not to move into leadership in ministry.

The rate at which the release should occur ought to depend on the ability of the emerging leader to pick up responsibility for it and not an authoritarian posture or a quick release posture. The arrow moving to the left demonstrates that the emerging leader should be picking up responsibility for the tasks, roles, or functions. As this is done, the leader should be releasing.

Overlap is that unique time in a leadership transition when the emerging leader and existing leader share responsibility and accountability for tasks, roles, and functions. It is the time in which both the leader and emerging leader are working together in an increasing way to release and accept responsibility. Overlap can occur anywhere along the continuum.

Tandem training describes the training technique during overlap used by an existing leader with an emerging leader. Tandem training allows the younger leader to share the learning experiences of the older leader via modeling, mentoring, apprenticeship, or internships so as to leapfrog the younger leader's development.

There are numerous instances in Scripture of leadership transitions. Most are not ideal as suggested by the transitional continuum. The Moses/Joshua transition which took place over an extended time does follow the description given above of the transitional continuum. It is one of the positive models of leadership transition in the Scriptures. Another positive model occurs in the New Testament - that of Barnabas and Saul.

Other leadership situations in Scripture are worthy of study, mostly for the negative lessons and identification of the items on the transitional continuum that are missing. Chart 9 lists some of the instances of Scripture that provide data for observing the positive and negative effects of leadership transitions - be they good of bad.

Chart 9. Some Instances in Scripture for Seeing Transition Insights

Joseph (sovereign transition)

Moses (sovereign transition)

Moses/Joshua (toward tandem transitions)

Joshua/? (none)

Eli/sons (negative)

Samuel (sovereign transition)

Samuel/Saul (modified negative)

Jephthah (other judges)

David/Absalom (aborted)

David/Solomon (negative)

Elijah/Elisha (minimum)

Daniel (sovereign)

Jesus/disciples

Apostles/deacons (Acts 6)

Acts 20 Paul/Ephesian elders

Saul/David (negative)

In the Moses/Joshua transition several steps, stages, or discernible events can be ordered. These give insights into why the transition was successful and led to a great leader being raised up to follow a great leader. The following are some observations which suggest why the transition was successful.

1. There was deliberate and definite leadership selection. Moses chose Joshua. Joshua came from a leading family with leadership heritage (note the march order in Exodus - his grandfather prominent).

2. Moses gave him ministry task with significant responsibility:

   a. first - select recruits and lead battle among the Amalekites who were harassing the flanks of the exodus march.
   b. second - spy out the land (probably one of the younger ones to be chosen). Moses checked Joshua's: a. faith, b. faithfulness, c. giftedness (charismatic ability to lead) with these increasing responsibilities.

3. Moses included Joshua in his own spiritual experiences with God. Joshua had firsthand access to Moses vital experiences with God. Moses took him into the holy of holies, frequently into the tabernacle into the presence of God, up on the mountain when he was in solitude alone with God. This was tandem training in spirituality using mentoring.

4. Moses recognized the complexity of the leadership situation toward the end of his life. He knew Joshua could not do it all. When transitioning him into leadership he saw that Joshua was a charismatic militaristic leader but was not the spiritual leader. He set Eleazar as the spiritual leader. He publicly did this - bolstered Eleazar in the eyes of the people, recognized Joshua's strengths and weaknesses. Moses knew that any leader coming into his position would have trouble - most likely could not fill his shoes; he would need help.

5. Public recognition. Moses recognized the importance of followers knowing whom he had appointed to be the next leader. No ambiguity. No scramble of leaders for that position after Moses' death. He settled it ahead of time and gave a public ceremony stipulating his backing of Joshua.

6. The new leader following an old leader must not look back and compare. One way of overcoming this tendency is to have a big challenge, a new task not done by the old leader. There was a big task to do. It would be his own contribution - possess the land.

7. The new leader needed to know not only that Moses had appointed him as leader but that God had confirmed this appointment. Deut. 31:14-18 and Joshua 1 point out Joshua's experiences personally with God concerning the appointment.

8. Not only must there be personal assurance that God has the appointment but there must be public recognition of this. God gives this in Joshua 3 (note Joshua 3:7, "What I do today will make all the people of Israel begin to honor you as a great man, and they will realize that I am with you as I was with Moses." See also Joshua 4:14, "What the Lord did that day made the people of Israel consider Joshua a great man"). They honored him all his life, just as they had honored Moses.

9. A leader moving into full responsibility needs an initial success that can bolster spiritual authority and demonstrate that the leader can get vision from God in his/her own right. Joshua's experience with the Captain of the Lord's Army was a pivotal point that did this. It gave him vision - tactical plan with strategic implications. Its success came early on and stimulated followers. With it there was assurance that brought closure to the whole transition experience.

10.A final thing that ensured a successful transition was the early failure - Ai. Leaders must know they are not infallible. They must trust God in their leadership. An early failure after initial success was a major deterrent to pride, showed the moral implications of Godly leadership, and the notion that leaders must always move followers along toward God's purposes for them in God's way.

This model has peculiar dynamics associated with it which may preclude its application in other situations. There was a long period of overlap due to the disciplining of the people in the wilderness. Joshua essentially led the next generation - not the one in which he and Caleb were members. There was a mighty expectation of a new task that challenged. He was from within (a home grown leader, from leadership heritage) and had proved himself in many ways before the followers. He was a charismatic/military leader with a good spiritual track record of sensing and obeying God. Certain of the underlying ideas of these observations will probably be applicable even if the overall dynamics are not identical.

BIBLIOGRAPHY

Blain, Hugh J.
1953   "Joshua." In *New Bible Commentary*. Francis Davidson, ed. Grand Rapids: Eerdmans Publishing Co.

Clinton, James Robert
1988   *The Making of A Leader*. Colorado Springs: Navpress.
1989   *Leadership Emergence Theory*. Altadena: Barnabas Resources.

Collingridge, Rich
1987   "Joshua." Pasadena: School of World Mission, Fuller Theological Seminary. Unpublished paper dealing with Joshua and leadership development.

Damazio, Frank
1987   *The Making of A Leader*. Eugene: Church Life Library.

Davis, Dale Ralph
1988   *No Falling Words*. Grand Rapids: Baker Book House.

Davis, John James
1969   *Conquest and Crisis*. Grand Rapids: Baker Book House.

Douglas, Principle
nd   *Joshua*. Edinburgh: T&T Clark.

Geikie, Cunningham
1896   *Old Testament Characters*. London: Longmans, Green, and Co.

Good, E.M.
1962   "Joshua Son of Nun," In *The Interpreter's Dictionary of the Bible*. Emery Stevens Bucke, ed. New York: Abingdon Press.

Gove, Philip Babcock, ed.
1981   *Webster Third New International Dictionary*. Springfield: Merriam-Webster Inc., Publishers.

Gowman, John Wick
   1962   "The Letter to the Hebrews, The Letter of James, The First and Second Letter of Peter." In *Layman's Bible Commentary*, vol. 24. London: SCM Press LTD.

Hamlin, John
   1983   "Joshua." In *International Theological Commentary*. vol. 6. George A. F. Knight and Frederick Carlson Holmgren, eds. Grand Rapids: William B. Eerdmans Publishing Co.

Hollander, Edwin P.
   1978   *Leadership Dynamics*. New York: The Free Press

Hughes, Kent
   1987   *Living On the Cutting Edge*. Westchester: Crossway Books.

Hyde, Douglas
   1966   *Dedication and Leadership*. Notre Dame: University of Notre Dame Press.

Jacobs, J. O.
   1970   *Leadership and Exchange In Formal Organizations*. Virginia: Human Resources Research Organization.

Judge, E. A.
   1988   "Slave, Slavery." In *The Illustrated Bible Dictionary*, part 3. J. D. Douglas, organ. ed. Sydney: Hodden Stoughton.

Kitchen, K. A.
   1988   "Egypt." In *The Illustrated Bible Dictionary*, part 1. J. D. Douglas, organ. ed. Sydney: Hodden Stoughton.

Kouzes, James M. and Barry Z. Posner
   1987   *The Leadership Challenge*. San Francisco: Jossey-Bass Publishers.

La Sor, William Sanford
   1946   *Great Personalities of the Old Testament*. Their Lives and Times. New York: Fleming H. Revell Co.

Montefiore, Hugh
    1964   "The Epistle to the Hebrews." In *The Harper's New Testament Commentaries*, vol. 14. New York: Harper & Row Publishers.
Moody, Dwight Lynman, T. DeWitt Talmage, and Theodore Parker
    nd   *Bible Characters*. Grand Rapids: Zondervan Publishing House.

Noth, Martin
    1962   *"Exodus."* In The Old Testament Library. Ernest Wright, John Bright, James Barr, and Peter Ackroyd, gen. eds. :SCM Press, LTD.

Rea, J.
    1975   "Joshua." In *The Zondervan Pictorial Encyclopedia of the Bible*. Merrill C. Tenney, gen. ed. Grand Rapids: Zondervan Publishing House.

Robinson, George Livingston
    1955   *Leaders of Israel*. Grand Rapids: Baker Book House.

Schaeffer, Francis A.
    1975   *Joshua and the Flow of Biblical History*. London: Hodder & Stoughton.

Smalley, Gary and John Trent
    1986   *The Blessing*. Nashville: Thomas Nelson Publishers.

Tichy, Noel M., and David O. Ulrich
    1984   "SRM Forum: The Leadership Challenge: A Call For the Transformational Leader. *Sloan Management Review*, fall: 59-68.

Vincent, Marvin R.
    1914   "The Synoptic Gospels, Acts of the Apostles, Epistles of Peter, James and Jude. In *Word Studies In the New Testament*, vol. 1. New York: Charles Scribner's Sons.

Waltke, B. K.
    1982   "Joshua" In *The International Standard Bible Encyclopedia*. Geoffrey W. Bromiley, gen. ed. Grand Rapids: Eerdmans Publishing Company.

Wiesel, Elie
1981   *Five Biblical Portraits*. Notre Dame: University of Notre Dame Press.

Young, E. J.
1988   "Ephraim." In *The Illustrated Bible Dictionary,* part i. J. D. Douglas, organ. ed. Sydney: Hodden Stoughton.

BARNABAS PUBLISHER'S MINI CATALOG

(Book Titles are in Bold and Paper Titles are in Italics with Sub-Titles and Pre-Titles in Roman)

BARNABAS   PUBLISHERS

Unique Leadership Material that will help you answer the question:
"What legacy will you as a leader leave behind?"

"The difference between leaders and followers is perspective. The difference between leaders and effective leaders is better perspective."
Barnabas Publishers has the materials that will help you find that better perspective and a closer relationship with God.

BARNABAS   PUBLISHERS
Post Office Box 6006 • Altadena, CA 91003-6006
Fax Phone (626)-794-3098 • Phone (626)-584-5393

Printed in the United States
36359LVS00007B/3-52